Willie Mae

ELIZABETH KYTLE

Willie Mae

With a foreword by Joyce A. Ladner
and an introduction by the author

Brown Thrasher Books

The University of Georgia Press
Athens and London

Published in 1993 as a Brown Thrasher Book
by the University of Georgia Press, Athens, Georgia 30602
© 1991 by Elizabeth Kytle

Original design and typography by George Salter
Printed and bound by Thomson-Shore, Inc.

The paper in this book meets the guidelines for
permanence and durability of the Committee on
Production Guidelines for Book Longevity of the
Council on Library Resources.

Printed in the United States of America

97 96 95 94 93   P   5   4   3   2   1

Library of Congress Cataloging in Publication Data

Kytle, Elizabeth.
    Willie Mae / Elizabeth Kytle : with a foreword by Joyce A. Ladner
and an introduction by the author.
    p. cm.
    "Brown thrasher books."
    Originally published : New York : Knopf, 1958.
    ISBN 0-8203-1518-4 (pbk. : alk. paper)
    1. Workman, Willie Mae. 2. Afro-Americans—Georgia—Biography.
3. Afro-American women—Georgia—Biography. 4. Segregation—
Georgia. 5. Afro-Americans—Georgia—Social life and customs.
6. Georgia—Biography. 7. Georgia—Social life and customs.
I. Title.
[E185.97.W8K98 1993]
975.8'00496073'0092—dc20
    [B]   92-28227
                                                         CIP

British Library Cataloging in Publication Data available

To Calvin,

and

to all the Willie Maes

Foreword by Joyce A. Ladner

I first read *Willie Mae* when I was a college student in Mississippi in 1964. It reminded me of the strong black women in my own family.

These were women who entered the work world in the kitchens of white women, some of whom were kind but most of whom were not. They were from the generation of women I call "do-ers."

These uneducated but extraordinarily resourceful women had been taught by their mothers and fathers to do whatever had to be done, whether relatively simple but hard tasks like cooking, ironing, sewing, and cleaning house, or difficult, complicated tasks like raising children—their own as well as those of their employers. Hard tasks and challenging events had forced them to play flexible gender roles. These same tasks and events, together with an unshakable faith in God, had forged within them a toughness of character and an optimistic spirit that the young of my generation found hard to comprehend.

DR. LADNER, a sociologist, is vice president for academic affairs at Howard University in Washington, D.C. She is the author of *Tomorrow's Tomorrow: The Black Woman* (Doubleday, 1971), a study of the impact of race and class on the development of black teenage girls.

Like all these do-ers, Willie Mae drew naturally on the traditions of her foremothers who, amid the horrors of slavery, fought valiantly to maintain a semblance of family life. It was a distinctly uneven fight. Through the commerce of slavery, husbands and wives were separated, and young children were often torn from their mothers' bosoms. Denied the right to worship their ancestral gods, they were permitted to practice Christianity only under the watchful eyes of the slaveowners. They were neither allowed to speak their own languages nor given opportunity to learn correct English. The system was organized and operated to deprive them of their very humanity. That it did not is enduring testimony to their determination, their integrity, and their ingenuity.

The necessity to remain resilient, to resist the influences of an oppressive, white-controlled society, did not, of course, cease with the end of slavery. And it is in the historical context of post-Reconstruction that we are introduced to Willie Mae.

Willie Mae was thirteen when her mother died. Not more than two or three years later, her father died. He had held the family together, financially and emotionally, through a failed second marriage and a move to Kentucky, but once he had a serious injury and Willie Mae went to work because her help was needed. Later, after his death, she was thrust, on the edge of adolescence, almost permanently into the role of "woman-child," a role for which her preparation had been brief but which she would accept without a whimper. With younger children in the family, she knew that she had no alternative: she had to become a do-er. It was then that she began her virtually life-long odyssey through the homes of one white family after another.

Through Willie Mae's life experiences—so faithfully captured and distilled in this first-person biography by Elizabeth Kytle—we see these Southern whites through the eyes of a black woman whose perception is colored not only by pain and adversity but by her unwavering view that she will ultimately prevail despite all the setbacks and all she has to put up with. In the telling, she demystifies white people, something I now recognize as a major contribution of the book. I grew up believing that most white people were racists and therefore alike. Willie Mae was wiser. She saw her white employers as individuals and, in a few telling and graphic phrases, fixes them in the reader's mind. ("He was the sorriest man God ever strung a gut to," she says of a well-to-do white who'd spoken disparagingly of President Roosevelt.) Willie Mae's insight served her as a survival skill, and she came early to distinguish between the overt and the subtle characteristics of the human personality. The white people in her life had their strengths and their weaknesses. Some were decent and treated her like a fellow human being; others were full of hate. She gives them all their due. At times I was angry at the conditions she faced, when she was not. I wanted to strike out at the despicable people who used her so cruelly. She never did. Unfailingly, she rose above the mean and small-minded, and in time moved on.

I now realize that it was only in the second reading of this book—twenty-five years after I first read it—that I really understood Willie Mae. When I was twenty I was not fully capable of comprehending her story, or my grandmother's. My own youth, inexperience, and lack of wisdom in the complexities and nuances of life caused me to view Willie Mae as another of the downtrodden black women who had, in part, allowed her labor to be exploited by evil white people. I wanted her to strike out, to rise up and protest against the inhuman conditions inflicted upon her, just as the poor black men and women with whom I was working in the civil rights movement were doing. But today I realize that Willie Mae did strike out in her own fashion and was no less effective than the civil rights activists a few decades later. Each generation has its own way of coping with the peculiar conditions of its time. Willie Mae must surely be regarded as one who managed to balance the delicate act of survival with the maintenance of personal dignity in an era when simply to get through the day was for many blacks no minor achievement.

There is, I believe, a lot in *Willie Mae* of great value to yet another generation. As a story of courage and fortitude, it can surely be useful to young blacks facing seemingly insurmountable odds today. Above all else, Willie Mae demonstrates with sufficient clarity that poverty alone does not insure failure, that harsh conditions need not be the sole determinant of one's life chances. Now, at a time when there is much talk about a "permanent" underclass, Willie Mae challenges us to dismiss notions of permanence and inevitability. Ultimately, the lesson we should learn is that most individuals, despite social class and racial background, can to some important degree shape their own destinies. Achievement is not entirely dependent on structural opportunities.

Such structural opportunities for blacks have increased impressively since the sixties, and one cannot help wondering how far in life Willie Mae would have gone had she had the benefit of civil rights legislation and an education. In the light of certain current events, however, one can also wonder whether these legally protected opportunities have brought any significant reduction in racial prejudice. To the extent that blacks and whites still need to understand one another, Willie Mae's story— which is to say, Elizabeth Kytle's book—is as timely today as it was when it first appeared.

August 1990

Author's Introduction

"*Willie Mae* is not a 'race' book and it's not a 'woman's' book."

This was always my opening remark when I was speaking before groups in Ohio during 1959, the year after the book was first published. Thirty-three years later, in its renascence, I add that usage changes with passage of time, and it behooves those who were very young or yet unborn in the forties and fifties to bear this in mind as they read further.

"Black" is to race as "Methodist" is to religious denomination—originally flung in derision, later seized by those taunted and fixed upon as a designation to be worn with appropriate self-esteem. In 1946, when I made a trial effort—abandoned but resumed ten years later—in the direction of a book, "black" was not a word for polite reference to race.

In Georgia, where Willie Mae and I lived at that time, "colored" and "Negro" were both used by blacks and whites; but "colored" was falling from favor, regarded more as old-fashioned than rude, and with both races "Negro" was most often used and considered courteous. "Black" had a history of hurtfulness and insult. In the mid-forties, in Atlanta at least, many blacks were highly sensitive to gradations of color, and when marriage partners were chosen, "light" mates were much prized because—it was no secret—lightness was a status symbol. In 1958, when *Willie Mae* was published by Alfred Knopf, "black" had appeared in the courteous vocabulary but "Negro" was still preferred. "Negro" phased out slowly as "black" progressed to its ascendancy, which wasn't reached until well into the sixties.

All the foregoing is by way of explaining why readers will find "colored" in *Willie Mae* (It was the word Willie Mae used) and both "Negro" and "black" in quotations from a paper I wrote in 1959.

Though emphatically not simply what was called a "woman's book," *Willie Mae* was more than somewhat offered as such to the public. The dust jacket carried warmly welcomed endorsements, from women only—Anya Seton, Mrs. George Marshall, Faith Baldwin, and May Sarton—along with rather sentimental copy that gave no hint of the ugly truths unveiled in the book. This puzzled me at the time but, looking back, I hazard the guess that it was an effort to block pre-judging and pre-rejection. Any publisher, any author, hopes for a fair hearing before judgment, and the social climate of the fifties was not such that a story of the deep South, that of a black woman's life and hard times, culminating in her burgeoning minimal assertiveness, could be confidently expected to set well with the white book-buying public in South or North. A publisher does run risks in bringing out certain books, and I have ever since been filled with gratitude to Knopf for its willingness to take a chance on the combination of unheard-of author and unpopular subject—unpopular because unseasonable. Blessedly, *Willie Mae* was kindly received.

After *Willie Mae* was accepted but not yet published, I was occasionally asked if it was written in dialect, and later, even after they'd read it, a few referred to its idiom as dialect. Just in case there is anywhere some lingering residue of the same confusion: The speech in *Willie Mae* is *not* so-called dialect but is idiom common to blacks and whites in the rural South. It's not my own natural speech but, through conversation with Willie Mae, I became familiar with it and superficially fluent in it and I'm very fond of it. It's apt, succinct, expressive, and it makes a little picture every time. When Willie Mae says "I wouldn't trust him behind a broomstraw," that's idiom. For those who had difficulty differentiating between this and "dialect," I used to say that dialect looked like nothing more than bad spelling, idiom was Tennessee Ernie Ford (the then popular country singer). Ages before 1946, many white Southerners were acutely aware of the gross impropriety of dialect and found it offensive in the extreme. Employment of it in writing or storytelling was firmly repulsed on the same incontestable grounds that it would be today—that it automatically and inevitably pollutes material with condescension and ridicule.

Out of a scrupulous regard for Willie Mae's sensibilities

and to make certain that she had absolute knowledge of all that would appear in print, the manuscript was read to her line by line. She made no objection or correction, and expressed joy over what I had made from some of the things she had told me in our rambling exchanges. In 1957, race relations had not improved so much that it didn't occur to some to ask if I intended to put my own name on the book to come out the next summer. It had never crossed my mind to put anything else, but it certainly did cross my mind and Willie Mae's that it might be well not to use her surname, which, now that it can be told, was Wright. We were conditioned to fear that she could conceivably be harassed or intimidated in some way. When the book was in her hands, however—and it was a beautifully produced book—she found that silence was more than her flesh and blood could bear, and, going by what she said to me, she told everybody within earshot or who had a phone. To my knowledge the only unpleasantness she met with was a phone call some time later from someone Willie Mae took for white (a woman, a rank stranger to us both; who she was and how she identified Willie Mae, I never had a clue), wanting to know if Willie Mae was getting any part of the money the book earned. (She was.)

In talks about *Willie Mae*, having established at the outset that in my view it was neither a narrowly race nor woman's book but a human document, I went on with the paragraphs quoted below. I am lifting them and other quotations from a paper I wrote as an aide-mémoire on those occasions thirty-three years ago.

"It is the life story of an uncommonly admirable human being who, due to the same process of accident of birth that made each of us whatever we are, was born American, Southern, female, Negro. These factors shaped her life, to be sure. But in her reactions to the events of that life it's always her essential humanity that shows, and her race and sex are obviously subordinate.

"Most of it is literally true of a real person who told me about it herself. Much of it could be true of almost any Southern Negro woman now in her sixties. A tiny percentage of the book recounts actual incidents that in life happened to people other than those in the book. There is only the merest trace of invention, and even these few frail fictions are totally true in spirit. Knowing all this, the publishers found that the most nearly accurate description they could devise was 'first-person biography.'"

As I continued, I explained that the rationale for a book about an obscure Southern women by another obscure Southern woman was two-pronged: my "belief that most white Southerners simply do not know Negro Southerners and my feeling that in Willie Mae I did know a Negro, one "whose life was, alas, commonplace." I emphasized that I was speaking of *average white Southerners*. In our youth in Atlanta, my husband and I and our contemporaries were privileged to know older men and women, white and black, who had long been working quietly (which is not to say secretly) and tirelessly in their sustained commitment to the improvement of conditions relating to race. Their work was cut out for them, because " . . . average white Southerners, many of whom are basically well-meaning but not given to facing reality when it has to do with race, simply never have come to recognize the common humanity of white and black people." It was a tangled web they wove; many of these average white Southerners, "to whom Negroes remain as inscrutable as the sphinx, feel that they know Negroes very well indeed."

Some of what they "knew" was "a collection of myths and a string of group-within-a-group characteristics which are not truly race-linked. Such whites cling like barnacles to this body of misinformation with a self-preserving passion to 'know' what it has always been to their advantage to believe." What they are offering " . . . .sometimes innocently, which is to say ignorantly, is a counterfeit. They're offering the counterfeit of long-standing, familiar, even intimate, association for the genuine coin of insight." I readily conceded that they did have some facts in their arsenal, but were nonetheless "as wrong as wrong can be. A fact is a sometime thing, dangerous to fool around with unless you know what it means. If you take hold of a fact by the wrong end—or by the throat—it can do nothing but lead you to some eminently wrong conclusions. As for the whites who handle facts in this way, it isn't hard to see how basing an important part of daily behavior on a fistful of wrong conclusions affects the quality of their lives."

As this was all being said in Ohio and long ago, doubtless there were those who wondered why Southern whites wouldn't know Negroes when, after all, they'd been down there together for a long time. I thought it was because "certain areas of the conventional white Southern mind are numb, numb from lifelong brutally tight encasement in a system set up years ago by other whites who meant the system to restrict Negroes only. Of course it didn't work that way. Many swords are double-edged, and the sword of segregation was . . . mutually damaging. It's not only muscles that atrophy from disuse. You figuratively bind up the part of a mind that would let its owner see another person as a person—distinguishable from an animated household appliance, for example—and eventually that part of the mind doesn't work. And this disability, while of course not genetically heritable, is certainly inherited, by the handing-down process. Or to paraphrase a biblical line about grapes and teeth, the fathers have eaten loco weed and the children's minds are on edge."

In those Ohio talks I pointed out that lack of understanding wasn't peculiar to the South. To quote myself again, "I've lived in Columbus for nearly ten years now, and it seems to me that here whites know Negroes to the extent that it's possible to know people from whom they're essentially separated. I'm sure you appreciate that separation can be effected as thoroughly by custom as by law." I felt that from knowing Willie Mae I had gained some insight . . . "and my hope is that the Willie Mae in the book may do at least a little of the same for some others."

The nicest thing I know that it did for some others was done, to my astonishment, for some black pre-adolescents in New York. A mutual friend told a teacher whose pupils were poor but bright black children that there was a book she should read, *Willie Mae*. "Why, Sylvia," said the teacher, "I've been using that book for nine years." She said that the children told her in class discussions that what they got from *Willie Mae*, new to them, was that there had been, in the race's fairly recent past, blacks to be proud of—though all the world different from their own day's activists. I found that indescribably gratifying, as it had distressed and irritated me that some modern blacks, during a certain period, distanced and even seemed to want to ignore the contributions of unlettered and, on the surface, unimpressive blacks of the generations immediately preceding them. (Again, not a race-linked characteristic.) This was to deny their debt to the very blacks on whose shoulders they were standing, who, by doggedly surviving in devastating circumstances, had scratched out a toehold for descendants. Whether or not those black schoolchildren were fully aware of it, they were talking about their own grandparents and great-grandparents. They were talking about all the Willie Maes.

Elizabeth Kytle
July 1990

"Your grandmother was also there,
and no one has ever accused her of being bitter.
I suggest that the innocents check with her.
She isn't hard to find. Your countrymen
don't know that she exists . . . though she has
been working for them all their lives."

—JAMES BALDWIN, *The Fire Next Time*

Willie Mae

1

Things have come to a mighty sorry pass when here I am, at my age and in my condition, packing up every Lord's thing I own and fixing to leave Georgia for good and all.

It always has been a hard row to hoe for colored folks; but now Herman Talmadge has done got himself elected governor, it's the frying pan *and* the fire. One while here I thought things might could get better, but now I know different. I'm solidly fed up.

I don't want nothing belongs to white folks. But I've plumb got a bellyful of the biggest portion of them treating us the way they do. Get on the bus, and nine times out of ten the driver looks at you like a snake done crawled on his bus—I sometimes wonder how does the Power Company find enough men mean enough to do their hauling—and people already on the bus shrinking away while you try to get to the back, looking like they'd sooner be in hell with both legs broke than have you so much as brush up against them. Which you wouldn't have to be pushing back to the back if the law didn't make you ride there. And people where you work at telling you it's perfectly all right for you to use their only toilet, just be real sure you lift the seat up first.

I'm slow to wrath, and I been getting the dirty end of the stick and keeping my mouth shut about it till I'm old and gray-headed, but now they've done gone too far. They sure tried themselves, seeing how much devilment could they do to scare colored folks out of voting. Fiery crosses in Jeffersonville and other places the night before the election, and Walton County——! Jesus God, they went to work a month ago in Walton County. Burnt up the Methodist church, burnt up the Baptist church, and then burnt up the schoolhouse. And then shot and killed my Cousin Walter down in Montgomery County because he did go and vote.

Some say Cousin Walter was the onliest colored person to vote in that county—I read about it in the Atlanta papers—and some say several hundred besides him voted, but they all say that when he went to the voting-place they told him he had a right to vote but if he was smart he wouldn't. He did though, and that night these two young white men come to his house and shot him to death.

They went free, of course. Oh, they had a trial, but I know how much that meant. They said they shot him in self-defense, because when they went to his house and called him he came out looking like he had a gun in his pocket. I don't know how does a man with a gun in his pocket look any different from a man without no gun, and I didn't see nothing in the papers 'bout they found a gun on his dead body. They shot him three times, on his own porch and with his wife and children looking on.

This puts the tassel on the cap. I hadn't seen Cousin Walter since he was a young kid—which he was only twenty-eight when they killed him—and I never was acquainted with his wife. He was only my second cousin; but, when this happened, it come over me all of a sudden that we were blood kin, and I reckon when they shot him they come pretty close to me. I can't study it out, and I know God has all the power—but sometimes it does seem God has pimps and pets.

Mrs. Carruthers don't know it, but she give me one last little push. I been minding her little boy off and on for three years and she always treated me very well, but it beats all what I heard her saying on the phone yesterday. I had always baby-sit by the evening for them and gone home when they come in. But this time her and Mr. Carruthers went off on a vacation trip and they got me to stay at their house to watch out for things and take care of the little boy. I didn't noways appreciate what she did, but they was all packed and ready to go and I just went on and held to my part of the bargain and stayed. I was turning it over in my mind all the while they was gone; and when I heard her talking about it on the phone, that did it.

She was talking to some friend she phoned up to say she

was just back from her trip, and, by my being right in the next room, I heard every word she said.

She said: "I declare, I just never will understand darkies. Willie Mae stayed here with little Don, you know, while we were away. Well, we're going to completely redo the guest room, so I said to her when we left, 'Willie Mae, I was going to make you a pallet, but you might as well sleep in the guest room. I'm going to send the mattress to be cleaned and recovered as soon as we get back home anyhow, and you may as well be comfortable.' And do you know what that silly thing said to me? She said she'd rather sleep on a pallet. And she did, too! Slept on a pallet she fixed herself and never went near the guest room! It's just beyond me. I've known darkies all my life, but I reckon I never will understand how their minds work."

Coming right on top of Cousin Walter, that got it started. Last night I commenced to pack, and soon as I get through I'm going to make tracks. I'm going to Washington where Mrs. Clifford is. I believe things will be better there, and she always said if ever I came there she'd sure get me a job. I been putting this off and putting it off, but no more —it's time to go.

A week ago you couldn't have told me *anything* could pry me loose from this housing-project, because it's been my world with a fence around it ever from that Sunday me and Viola picked out card No. 130. But, sweet Jesus, this state has done gone to pot, and I feel like they tore down my fence and trampled me like a posse ripping through a cornfield.

This gas-heated project saved my life last winter when I had the pneumonia. I all but know I would have died if I'd been living in a ramshackle place like the last place we had, that slum hole on Chestnut Street. Just the same, it don't do a body too much good to be warm in the winter and such as that if your very heart and soul gets stomped on twenty-odd times a day—and maybe a bullet through your head if you dast go out and vote like you think you're a regular human being. I never voted in my life, and I'm too ageable to start now; but them colored folks as knows what they're doing, they out to be let vote in peace. And get their votes counted, too.

First things I started packing were some bits and pieces of dishes and things that used to belong to Momma, way back there in Carrollton. I petted that little cut-glass bowl in my hand—Momma used to love it so—and I thought about how us children used to love to thump it with our finger to hear it ring. Momma never minded us doing that, either; she liked to hear it ring her own self, because she said that was how you could always tell was a dish real cut glass or no.

This ain't the first time I've thought of Carrollton. Ever since Joyce married Gerald, and that left just me and Viola, I've thought about the country a lot. Sometimes I almost used to wish I still lived in the country instead of Atlanta, and there's times when I long for a wood stove to cook with and a fireplace. When I was little, all our family used to sit around the fireplace at night and we'd make wishes on the sparks that flew out. I'd purely love to tote in firewood, I'd be so glad if I had a fireplace. I ain't forgetting it was the gas-heater saved my life last winter. Still and yet, you can't make no wishes on a gas-heater.

And when I was out by Dunwoody the other day and saw all that cotton growing, I wanted to go to Carrollton so bad I could taste it. I used to be a cotton picker for white folks when I was a little girl in Carroll County. I looked at those fields out by Dunwoody, and I knew that by September they'd be white as snow. I got it in mind to go out there then and pick some cotton, even if it was for just one hour and no pay—for old time's sake. Yes, long before I wrapped Momma's cut-glass bowl good and thick in newspaper and put it in the barrel, Carrollton kept staying on my mind.

2

When I was a child, I was the biggest jackass in Carroll County. I stayed the baby for nine years and I didn't walk till I was seven, so quite naturally I was spoiled.

There was two brothers and two sisters ahead of me. Each one of us was about two years older than the next one, except for Florrie and Jeanette. They was the youngest. Emma was the oldest and the meanest. We called her Sister, and she was the big shot of the family. Lee come next, and he was as sweet as Sister was mean. Then come Jessie, and she was really too good to be a human. We called her Baby. Then come Buddy, then me. There was nine years between me and Florrie; and two years after Florrie, Jeanette come.

We lived in Gruber's Grove. It was a pretty grove—oak trees in front and a pine thicket in back. There was three houses in the Grove. We lived in the largest one. It was a four-room house and we paid three dollars a month rent.

The three families that lived in Gruber's Grove used the same well, and Mr. Gruber had fixed it so the well wasn't no farther from one house than it was from another. He was a German man, and he was very wealthy. Carrollton was really owned by three rich families—the Grubers, the Aikens, and the Ambersons. The Aikens and the Ambersons owned factories, and Mr. Gruber owned and rented out a lot of property.

We had a two-horse wagon and two mules. We had two cows, passels of hogs—I remember one old sow that had fifteen pigs in one litter—and chickens, turkeys, and ducks. Dogs and cats, too. We had a cat hole in every door but the front door. Folks won't let you cut cat holes in their doors now but then they did, and Poppa just used to cut a small square right in the corner of a door.

Momma always had a little garden plot, with old-timey flowers like roses and violets. She was crazy about different kinds of lilies, and we always had them. And then there was the four o'clocks, bushes with little sweet-smelling pink and white flowers that opened up at four o'clock every afternoon. We used to string these, right close together, on a long string from some kind of weed, knot the ends of the weed together, and hang them around our necks.

Saturday was clean-up day. We'd scour and wash and get ready for Sunday. We didn't know nothing about no mops like we have now. We'd take corn shucks and put them in a piece of wood and make a scrub brush. For the soap, we'd save all old fat meat and all kinds of greases and take the ashes from oak wood and make lye out of it. You pour water over the oak ashes, let that water run off; that's lye water, and it's the color of dark tea. Put that in the pot with the grease and a ball of potash, and that's the best soap that's ever been on the market. It's not to bathe with, just for washing and scrubbing, but it makes the prettiest white floors you ever saw.

It was a long time before I helped with any of that though, because I didn't walk until I was seven years old. It's a place on my heel now about as big as a quarter and it's blue under my skin, and every time I ever went to the Grady here in Atlanta the doctor looked at it. One doctor said: "You was a long time about walking, wasn't you?" I wondered why he asked me that, and he said it was on account of that place on my heel, and mine was only the second one he had ever seen. He said it was something about the leaders in my leg, and he said I did good to walk at seven.

The way I first started walking was a show train come to town. We lived near a railroad track, and if a circus train would be coming in or something like that we'd have five or six families come to our house so they could watch it go by. One day they was all out in the yard looking, and I was in the house. Poppa was sitting in the back door and I heard him say: "Here it come now!" With that everybody jumped up and ran out to look, and I jumped up and ran too. I went through two rooms and to the back door and looked out at that train.

Momma just clean forgot to rejoice about the circus train and kept saying: "My baby's walking! My baby's walking!" Poppa was happy too, and he kept saying: "Willie Mae, let's see you walk some more." And I walked around the house so much that all at once my legs folded up under me and I sit on the floor.

Momma sent for Dr. Pitt, and he come. He was a white doctor, and he had an old black buggy and a white horse. Momma told him what happened, and he'd tell me to get up and I'd try. I'd get up, too, but I'd go right back down to the floor. He'd push at me some, and then he'd tell me to come and get things he'd hold out to me, but I couldn't make it. Finally he said: "Well, when the time comes for her to walk again, she'll walk."

I was poor as a snake; I don't believe I hardly weighed fifty pounds. I had real long hair, and Dr. Pitt said it was taking my strength. I don't remember the next time I walked, but I just learned gradually. I used to catch hold of chairs and the side of the house and help myself get around that way. When I got so I could do a little better, I used to push chairs in front of me and go along that way. Momma never could keep a rug straight for me doing that.

When I did start walking I could walk just a little, not like other folks. After I got to hobbling around a little bit, they got me a billy goat and wagon—the cutest little green wagon. Then I could go around just as good as anybody. Weren't any cars to be afraid of, there was just buggies then.

One day, as the Lord would have it, Carrollton was full of gypsies. They must have started from the center of town, like they always do, and spread out. Them gypsies saw me coming down the road in my billy-goat wagon, and they overtook me. They taken me out of my wagon and all but throwed me in their wagon. What made me so mad, they put an old nasty stinking quilt over my face. Lord, I hollered and prayed and moaned and called Momma. I thought they was going to kill me. When they didn't, I started saying I wanted my goat and wagon. I told them I couldn't hardly walk and that's why I had to have the goat and wagon back. One of the gypsy women said: "Well, if she can't walk, she's no good. Put her out." So they stopped on the side of the road, and where they put me out at there wasn't no house for miles. Three or four miles at least, it turned out.

I didn't know which way I was or what road I was on, and they had carried off my goat and wagon, and they only gave me a smutty-looking piece of bread to last me till I got home. At that time I couldn't walk, not and stand up good, the length of a room. I throwed the bread down and boohooed and bellowed.

I just sat there, crying down. Finally a colored and a white man come along together, and I told them what had happened. The white man said it was a dirty damn shame what they did to me. They carried me most of the way home, but I couldn't even make it the rest of the way. I'd walk a little bit and then rest a while. I come to some white people's house on the highway and made it in to the gate. I was crying so the white lady couldn't make no sense out of me. She was dipping snuff with a toothbrush, so I couldn't understand her either. She let me stay there all that night though; she let me sleep in the hall.

Next morning she was going to town, and she brought me and put me off right on the main highway. First somebody I seen was one of Poppa's best friends. He went to blessing me out about how my momma and poppa were half crazy with me gone all night; but when I told him what a time I had, he helped me get home.

I worried and I cried and stomped and went on about my billy goat. Then Mr. Gruber found out I'd done got home and he come down to see us and to give me a quarter. He was nothing but a millionaire. He was old, but he stood straight as a stick. He was tall, but he was skinny— no bigger than your arm, the littlest white man I ever saw. Well, when he found out what had happened to my goat and wagon he didn't say anything, but a couple of nights later he came back leading the cutest little brown-and-white spotted pony I ever saw. Somebody else give me a buggy then, and I was the first colored girl in Carroll County had a horse and buggy.

On account of the Grubers were so good to me, I named the pony Nell—for Mrs. Gruber. All the little white girls in Carrollton commenced to play with me then, because they liked to ride in my buggy. Some of them had wealthy parents and they had plenty of money to buy a

horse and buggy; still and all, for a long time I was the
only child, white or colored, that had one.

*   *   *

Maybe a year or so after that I got so I could walk right
good, and it was then I started picking cotton. Poppa most
usually did construction work, but some years he'd farm;
and when he did, Momma and Little Buddy and me would
work for him. His farm was out in the country a right
smart piece. It wasn't really none of his farm, but he used
to rent it. We'd get up in the morning about four o'clock,
no later than five ever, and go pick cotton. Some mornings
it would be so dark that we'd light pine knots and stick
them in trees to see to pick by.

When Poppa would be doing construction work, he'd
be off in town. He'd get jobs like digging ditches and he'd
hire men to do the digging. Sometimes he'd be gone a week
or two weeks on his jobs; and that's when Momma and
Little Buddy and me would pick cotton for white folks.
Looks like that's how I remember Buddy best, picking cotton alongside me and cracking jokes. We called him Little
Buddy because he was thin and frail-looking, but he wasn't
really frail or sick a lot. He just never did eat like other
boys. When he would eat, he'd eat a lot of foolishness. He
sure was a clowner; he was up to something all the time
and just loved to tease folks. He was bright too, just as
quick as a squirrel after a nut. The white folks we picked

cotton for would send a wagon to pick up all their hands, and you could hear the wagons start rolling about three in the morning. Buddy would stand in the door and listen. Then I'd hear him say: "There goes Mr. Hall's wagon," or "Here comes Mr. Smith's wagon—you all better come on." I never could do that about wagons, but I can learn anybody's walk.

One man was having trouble getting his cotton picked. He couldn't get any help. Then he got smart. He went and got a truck. That was the first truck we ever seen in the country, and when he come around in his truck everybody wanted to pick for him to get to ride in the truck. They never had rode in anything that pulled by gasoline. He got his cotton picked before anybody else that year.

Same as I was late picking cotton, I sure was the cow's tail about going to school—on account of me taking so long about walking. I was nearly nine before I started to school.

It wasn't nowhere hardly from home. We just had to go across the railroad tracks and through a cornfield. It was just one old big room, made out of big logs. It had a big heater right in the middle of it, and all the boys had to tote up firewood and pile it in the back corner of the room. There was around about fifty of us in that room, and classes went up to the fourth grade, and Professor Hardy was the only teacher. The fifth, sixth, and seventh grades was in another little building.

Professor Hardy would give us reading in the morning and spelling in the evening, all out of the same book. We didn't have but one book; it was a little brown-backed reader. Professor Hardy would say: "First grade, pass up side of the wall." And all us in the first grade would get up and come out of our seats and line up. He'd tell us what page to turn to, and then he'd start at the head of the line. Everybody would read so much, however much he told us. Whenever there'd be spelling, he'd call out the words. If the first one couldn't spell her word, he'd send her to the foot of the line and go on to the next one. I never got nowhere with spelling, but I'd walk away with the others in reading.

In spelling, we'd have our books shut up, but I'd be bad about peeping. I can hear him now, saying: "Apple, Willie Mae Cartwright." And the next thing I'd hear would be somebody yelling out: "She's peeping!"

We didn't start using tablets until the second or third grade. I done very well with writing, but I couldn't write straight unless I had lines.

The boys sit on one side of the room and the girls on the other. If Professor Hardy would catch us talking, he'd make us stand on one foot for so many minutes with a bucket of water in our hand. Oh, we'd be so shaking, and I'd spill more water on the floor. I'd always get caught talking; every day and sometimes twice a day. I didn't care about school nohow; I wanted to work. I just liked the name of going to work, even before I was old enough to go to school. If I could have gone earlier, like the other children did, I might have been all right.

Besides me not caring about school, we didn't learn nothing there nohow. Professor Hardy was very well, but his wife was so mean. He'd send two or three of us every day over to his house to tend to the children and wash up the dishes. We didn't know no better and we were glad to do it to get out of school, but that's why we couldn't learn nothing. He'd say: "Aline, Willie Mae, Laura: You girls stand and pass over to Mrs. Hardy's." Couldn't none of us stand her, she was so hateful, but we didn't have the mother wit to rather stay in school. My job was mostly to tend to the children. Aline would wash the dishes and Laura would clean up. Mrs. Hardy would lay down and take a nap. Then she'd give us an apple or something to get on our good side and tell us not to tell Professor Hardy she didn't hear us our spelling.

They didn't teach nothing like cooking in school then, just book learning. But now children has moving-picture shows and gym and all that mess, and then go to the show again when they get out of school. We didn't have but one show, and that was the circus that come once a year. Now and then sometime a carnival would come in town. Everybody and his brother would be there to the carnival. Another time there was something in Burnsville almost as good as the circus. A man come there with a wagonload of bananas, and he had this rooster with him what had sandy long hair, just like white people's, instead of feathers. The man had it fixed so you couldn't see the rooster until you bought some bananas. We all got our little money and went to see the rooster—Burnsville wasn't noways from Carrollton—and I seen him. He was a real rooster all right, but later on we heard they had fastened a little wig on his head some way.

When I was round about ten, I got my first regular job —nursing for Miss Annie Lois Brooks. She had the only automobile in town, a little red-seated one. It was a Ford, of course, and I'll never forget it. One day she brought me home in the Ford. She didn't carry me all the way down in the Grove, but put me out on the highway. I didn't know the car would stop completely, and I thought when it slowed down I had to jump out. So when she slowed down I did jump out, and I leapt right in a ditch and hurt my arm real bad. I have the scar till now.

I couldn't work for a long time after I hurt my arm. My poppa was mad with my momma for letting me go up to the Brookses and work anyhow. All I made was fifty cents a week.

Come to think of it, that was really the second little job I had. The first one was to tend to a little boy named Leland, and I had made twenty-five cents a week on that.

Every Saturday when I'd get that quarter I'd be so scared I'd lose it I'd think up different ways to carry it home. I'd put it in my dress pocket, I'd put it in my shoe,

I'd put it down in my stocking, and sometimes I'd just carry it tight in my fist. I'd give Momma the quarter, and she'd give me back a dime.

One Saturday I took the dime and bought a pocket-book, and that was the first pocketbook I ever had. It was a little old round pocketbook; it was soft and had pockets in the sides; it didn't have any drawstring, just mashed shut. When Momma saw it she said I'd bought a man's pocket-book, but I didn't care. Course I'd spent my dime to get it and didn't have any money in it.

I used to run to meet Poppa when he came home from work, and that day I said: "Look, Poppa, what I got!" I showed him the pocketbook. He looked and said: "Well, you ain't got nothing in it." I said no, that I just had a dime and that's what the pocketbook cost. He said: "Well, don't never spend your last cent for a pocketbook and it empty. You should have saved your dimes two or three weeks, and then you'd have a pocketbook with money in it."

I had a little blue tintop trunk where I kept my clothes. I put the pocketbook on the bottom of the trunk, under my clothes. Once when I went to look at it, it wasn't there. I nearly fell out for dead. Then I just knew Buddy had taken it. I tore up to the store where he worked, but he was out on a delivery trip. I was cutting up and carrying on something awful. I was so mad I nearly 'bout had a fit, and I kept yelling: "Buddy stole my pocketbook!"

When I went on home I told Momma about it, and she said I didn't have any business telling Mr. Evans and them

other white folks that Buddy had stole my pocketbook.
"Now they'll be accusing him of stealing at the store," she
said. I know most that they did, but I didn't know any better than to say what I did. I wouldn't say that kind of thing
nowhere now. But then I kept on fussing and hollering
and going on. Buddy had taken the pocketbook, and I got
it back. He had put two nickels in it and Momma let me
keep the money, being as he'd taken my pocketbook and
told a lie about it.

I put a nickel in church the next day. We used to belong
to the Mt. Vernon Baptist Church, and we went to church
every Sunday. I'd just have a fit if we ever didn't go. The
pastor was Reverend Smiley. Mt. Vernon was a big
white church on the other side of Carrollton from us. It
had just plain white windows at first, and green shutters.
Then later on they decided to have pretty windows, and
every member had to give so much to help pay for the
windows. The new windows had pictures of Christ and
other Bible pictures, and they were all in different colors,
looked like water colors. We thought we had the finest
church there was after we'd got the new windows. Then
they put green carpet all down the aisle. It sure was pretty
as a peach.

Sunday School was very unconvenient for us on account of the distance, but we always went to the eleven
o'clock service. If the buggy broke down we'd go with
neighbors, either go in the wagon. Sometimes we'd even
have to walk. If we started out walking, we'd have to leave

home round about eight or nine in the morning to get there for eleven o'clock service. We couldn't never make it walking to Sunday School, because we just wouldn't be there in time.

After church we'd go to BYPU and then stay for night service, and we wouldn't get home until nine-thirty or ten o'clock plenty of Sunday nights. We'd carry baskets of food and eat dinner on the grounds. The scaffolds they built the church with was still in the churchyard, and big stacks of planks. Each family would go and get planks and make tables; some were so long two or three families could spread on that one table.

Poppa would get up early Sunday morning and clean the buggy and brush up the horse and make her right slick, and clean the lines. During the week people drove with a rope, but on Sunday they had nice leather lines. We had a nice fast-trotting brown horse named Kate. And then one time we got a top for the buggy—a real good top, black leather with tassels all around it. The first Sunday we had it the sun wasn't shining at all, but Poppa went to putting the new top up anyhow. Momma said: "Name of God, Walt, we don't need that top up today." But Poppa wanted to let folks see he had done got a top for his buggy, so he put it up anyhow.

If we'd have to go to church in the wagon, I just couldn't stand it. Sometimes the buggy shaft would be broke down or Lee would be using the buggy. Poppa would let the older children use the buggy sometimes. Lee would want it for him and his girl, or he'd be taking some friends to Riverside or White Creek or some other church out in the country, and then we'd use the mule and wagon. That would just fly all over me. When we went by any big shot's house—any home-owner was a big shot—I'd lay down in the bottom of the wagon, Sunday clothes and all, so they wouldn't see me going to church in a wagon. Momma didn't like it either, but she wouldn't lay on the floor.

Sometimes we wouldn't stay to church all day because Poppa would have to take the Grubers out driving in their carriage. When he'd do that he'd wear the clothes Mr. Gruber gave him just to drive in. He'd have on black trousers or either hickory-striped trousers, and real good black shoes. His coat was frocktailed and the front was brocaded, and he wore a black bow tie. He had a high beaver hat with a rim around it. He had a heavy suit of mustaches, and he'd work on them till they were just as sharp. He wanted the ends to stick out right straight in points, and he'd twist them till they did.

Poppa looked good in those swanky clothes. He was tall and light-skinned, and he was broad-shouldered and heavy-built just like all his brothers. He could carry off those fine clothes, because he was sort of a big shot himself. He was the Keeper of Records and Seals for the Knights of Pythias, and he was very active in the Odd Fellows.

Sometimes we'd see Poppa carrying the Grubers in

after they'd been out to ride. He'd drive in through the big front gate on the prettiest white sandy road; wasn't no hard rocks, and you couldn't hear the horses trotting on it. We'd wait, and we could tell just as good when Mrs. Gruber was going to let Poppa carry us to ride. We could see him turning around, coming back out the gate instead of putting the coach in the carriage house. Miss Nell used to say: "Walter, would you like to carry Jennie and the children to ride in the carriage?" Which of course he always did, every chance he got. Mr. Gruber had two trim-built little black horses—not real black, but brown-black. One wasn't no bigger than the other; they was exactly the same size. Their tails was the bushiest tails, and they nearly touched the ground. And the carriage was the finest carriage I ever laid eyes on. It was black, and all inside there was little vases to put flowers in. All in the top was little silver tassels; and when you'd ride, the tassels would bounce. When we were out in it, I'd wave at everybody we'd see. I wanted to be seen. I'd put that big bow of red ribbon in my head and I'd always try to stick my head out the window, but Poppa wouldn't let me.

Momma and Buddy worked for the Grubers regular. Buddy used to get up and go over there every morning before he went to the store, and he'd make fires and shine shoes. He got a dollar a week for that. Momma was the Grubers' cook, and she really was a first-class cook. Momma was good and kind too and everybody was crazy about her, white and colored. She was real dark; none of us is as dark as Momma. She had coal-black hair and the evenest, whitest teeth you most ever seen.

Mrs. Gruber—we called her Miss Nell—told me to come up to the big house every day about twelve-thirty or one and get my dinner. Everybody in the country and little towns then eat exactly at twelve o'clock. After Momma and I had dinner I'd take the ashes out of the stove, sweep off the back porch, bring in the churning-cloths off the line, and help Momma get through. Then we'd go on home. Cooks went home after midday dinner in those days.

Whenever Poppa got a construction job outside of Carrollton the Grubers never did mind him leaving town on it, and he'd go back to working for them when it was finished. One time there was a big job of work for the county, and we looked for Poppa to get it because he was the onliest one asking for it that had his men all lined up to do the digging. He didn't though, and we heard tell that the county man that did the hiring said he wasn't going to hire no work gang except what had a white foreman. I know almost that Poppa didn't say a word to this man, because Poppa never was one to cut off his nose to spite his face, but he was madder about this than I ever seen him before or after. He was mad clean down to his gizzard, and that night he sat and stared into the fire so long till I wondered what could he see there.

He sat there and stared and stared and didn't say a word, and kept tapping his fist in the flat of his other hand. He was tapping his fist real easy and quiet—still and yet he was leaning forward and he had his teeth bit tight together and that little muscle in his jaw kept a-jumping. Finally he said—and he spoke quiet, too—"If we'd had any say-so in who county officers is, this wouldn't have happened." Momma almost jumped, and she couldn't have looked more scared if a thousand-leg had crawled up her neck. She told Poppa he hadn't ought to talk that way in front of the children, and he never did again; but once in a long while he'd say: "Well, Jennie, the day will come . . ." Momma'd always get that same special one expression on her face and look at him real hard and he'd stop every time, right in the middle. It was a right smart while before I caught on he was talking about voting; and when I did, Momma told me if I ever told anybody, white or colored, what he had said, she'd skin me alive.

After I'd stayed the baby nine years, here come Florrie. After that Momma didn't cook out any more, but she sewed at home. She used to make bonnets, the prettiest ones you ever seen, for grown folks and children too.

I had a blue one for every day. It had ruffles across the front and one in the back, and it tied in a bow under my neck. I'd call it gingham; they didn't know nothing about chambray then. There was narrow lace on the edge of the ruffle. My Sunday bonnet was solid white, but it had little squares in it.

Children then had to wear aprons. No matter what you

had on, you put a white apron over the top of it. I used to get so mad I wouldn't know what to do when I had to put that apron on over my pretty blue dress. The dress was gathered up on the shoulder and had ruffles coming over the shoulder and down the front. A sash was tacked on each side of my waist and it tied in the back with a big bow. The dress was just like pinafores children wear now except for the sash that tied from the sides—these pinafores have belts all the way around. The dress had ruffles around the tail too, and when I'd walk they'd bat around. But it wasn't no fun with an apron on. You couldn't switch your ruffles with an apron on, and so the dress didn't look pretty. Many a time I've taken my apron off after I left home and hid it under somebody's house.

Momma would have customers for her bonnets, and I'd go out and deliver them. Bonnets were all the go then, and everybody wore them—children, grownups, white and colored. A one-ruffle bonnet was thirty-five cents; the more ruffles they had the more they cost, and lace made them cost more too. But none cost more than a dollar, and Momma really made nice bonnets. She kept lots of cloth and lace and all such as that at home. She wouldn't let nobody bring their own cloth for bonnets; she'd let them pick out from the cloth she had.

Somebody, I don't remember was she white or colored, come to Momma for a bonnet, and said another woman had made her a fine bonnet for two dollars. She wanted another two-dollar bonnet. Momma told her she didn't know what kind of a bonnet that would be, for a high price like two dollars, so Momma asked her to bring it and let her see it. This woman brought the bonnet and Momma looked at it good. Momma said it wasn't worth it, but the woman said she wanted another two-dollar bonnet. Momma made one for her, and when she finished it she gave it to me and said: "Carry this bonnet over to that fool and let her part with her money." The customer was well satisfied with the bonnet because she'd paid two dollars for it, but Momma said it wasn't worth more than eighty-five cents or a dollar.

Momma made dresses too. Long about Easter-time and Christmas-time, she'd just have plenty of work to do. And she used to make beautiful quilts. She used to have big screws in the ceiling of the middle room. Poppa bore them up there for her to hang her quilts on, like cup-hooks. There was four poles to a quilting-frame, one for each side, and a rope on each corner. Several could quilt at the time. When they'd get ready to quit quilting for a while, they'd wind the quilt up. Somebody at each corner would untie the knots and wrap the rope around the pole, and that would draw the quilt up to the ceiling where it wouldn't be in the way. They used a good strong rope, a ply line is what it was; that's what everybody bought for quilting.

The biggest portion of people nowadays quilt on the bed, but you can't quilt on the bed as well as you can if the quilt is hanging from the ceiling. If you quilt on the bed, you can't keep it straight. A quilt has lining, then cotton, then the top, and you can't hold all that straight on the bed.

They didn't quilt with spool thread, either; they used ball thread. Penny a ball, five for a nickel. Momma used to make quilts to sell, and she'd get a dollar and a dollar and a half for them. We used to go to the mill and get sacks, ten for a dime. Then we'd go to the wash place, fill the iron pot with water, and build a fire. We'd take the lye soap we'd made and put it in the pot and wash them sacks out. Talk about something pretty and white! After they'd dried, we'd take them in the house by the fireplace. We had six big heavy smoothing-irons—we didn't know nothing about no electric irons—and we'd set them in front of the fire to get hot. Then we'd iron the sacks.

There's a certain way you can start ripping a sack and the thread will go all the way around. Momma used to rip them up that way and wind all that thread on a corncob or a stick and save it to quilt with. That would save her from buying ball thread. Me and Buddy always did wash the sacks for her; that was our job and we loved it. I just always did like to get in a tub and wash. I still do. We'd boil out the letters and printing on the sacks, and we had a battling-block. When there was still some print that wouldn't boil out, we'd reach down in the soap bucket and get lye soap and spread it all over the sack wherever the print still showed. Then we'd put it on this battling-block and beat it with a battling-stick, and when we'd get through beating there wouldn't be a letter left in the sack. We had the most fun beating those sacks.

But what we did to those sacks wasn't a circumstance to what Momma did to Miss Rachel. Momma heard Miss Rachel was going with Poppa, and she started watching out for them. One day she went down to the road and I went with her. I was still the baby then, and I always kept right up with Momma. We were standing under a big oak tree, and Momma had the battling-stick. It was about four feet long and half again as wide as your hand. We had done used it so much the handle was slick and smooth.

Directly, here come Poppa, hauling bricks for the Chattahoochee Brick Yard. We knew who it was soon as we saw the little red mule and the green wagon. And sitting up there beside Poppa, under a big parasol, was Miss Rachel. She was a big stout light-skinned woman, and she smoked cigarettes. That's how we first knew she was a rough-type woman.

They seen us, but Momma held the stick behind her and she never said a word to either one of them, so they come on. I think Poppa thought once that she might be meeting him to bring him his dinner, because all he said was: "Here's Jennie." Him nor Miss Rachel knew what Momma had it in mind to do, so he didn't attempt to turn off another way.

But when they got up close, Momma said to Miss Rachel: "You old heifer. Come on down off that wagon."

Then Poppa seen they was in for it and he began to get excited. He said: "You better get out and run, Rachel." She tried, but every whichway she tried to get off the wagon, Momma would head her off. She finally got down, and when she did she tore out running, but Momma caught her and like to beat her to death. I ran right along too, and I kept yelling: "Beat her, Momma!" I really didn't know what was it all about—women slipping with other women's husbands and all that stuff. I just knew if Momma was mad with her, I was too. Miss Rachel was just a-yelling, but wasn't nothing else for Poppa to do, so he drove off.

When he come home that night, Momma let him have it too. She practically busted him open with the same battling-stick. She fooled him, because she didn't bother him when he first come in. She waited till he took his clothes off, so he couldn't run out of the house. Then she just laid into him, and she was strong, too.

Men's underwear was long then, and they tied the legs around the ankles with strings. Poppa kept backing off from Momma and turning every whichway—he wouldn't fight back at her, he just kept trying to get away from her —and his strings was just a-flapping. I couldn't help laughing, he looked so comical. Buddy was the only one didn't want Momma to hit him. All us others wanted it. We were crazy about Poppa, but we loved Momma the best. I learned later it probably wasn't too much of Poppa's fault.

Miss Rachel was a bad woman, and she had ran at him for a long time.

When I was eleven or twelve I joined the church, but I didn't have no religion. I just joined like the other children did, to get near the water and to keep up with the others. After I got up some age, I realized what I'd done. It bothered me, and I was baptized again in Atlanta when I was forty or more—at Wheat Street Baptist, in that big glass pool.

But that first time was in Carrollton. The revival was running every night in the week for about a month, and a big baptizing at the end of it. A big old fat girl named Cora Hollingwood told us children to try and get religion and join. She said if you didn't join the church you'd go to the devil when you died. We'd promise her every day we'd join that night. Finally we did. We were all there on the benches way in the back.

When they opened the doors of the church for sinners to come up and pray, we all would get up and go shake hands with the preacher. Then we'd go down on our knees on the mourners' bench. Everybody's mother would come and pat us on the shoulder and we'd hear them saying things like "Trust God and get religion. Just trust Him. He'll help you. Just trust Him." We didn't know what was He going to help us about, but we reckoned we trusted Him. We'd whisper to each other—"Is you really going to join?" The mothers would be right down on top of us like a duck on a June bug. "Stop that whispering!" And we'd always say: "I'm not whispering. I'm praying."

Then we'd get up and sit on the same bench we'd been praying at, and everybody would go to singing again— "Jesus, Hold My Hand" and "Gimme That Old-Time Religion"—and the preacher would tell everybody to come up and accept God. The night I joined, I think there was around fourteen or fifteen of us. Momma jumped high as a wagon wheel when I joined; she was so excited she just shouted. We was candidates then for the water, and they appointed different folks to see after us. Mostly it was the candidates' mothers to see after them. Your mother would see to getting your things ready: a white outing robe, a long slip—they didn't want your legs to show—and for the Lord's sake, buy a brand-new towel, white with a red border. That was to keep your head from getting wet. They baptized at Amberson's Pond.

Sunday afternoon when they'd baptize looked like to me there'd be at least five to six hundred people, white and colored, at Amberson's Pond. The Pond was way cross town from the church, three miles or more. All of the candidates would have to go around to different people's houses to dress and undress, because they didn't have any place at the Pond.

A baptizing always started at three o'clock Sunday afternoon. Before that though, there'd always be one of the deacons to go out in the water to test the water, get rocks or glass or anything raked out of the way, see was there any snakes around, and find a good place where there wouldn't be any suck hole. He'd stick a stick up right where he was standing when he found a good place, to let the preacher know it was safe. He'd do that in the morning.

There wasn't twenty cars in Carrollton then, but there'd be buggies and two-horse wagons all around the Pond. It would scatter that there was going to be a baptizing, and everybody would come. If you didn't get there in time, you couldn't see. Some of the folks what got there late would climb up in trees. Everybody lined up and they'd all meet on the road and march, two by two, on down to the water, singing: "Take Me to the Water." You could hear everybody singing for three miles, I know. Baptizing used to be something then. They used to roll and tumble and shout.

Some would get in the water that wasn't being baptized. Lots of times men and women would get so happy when they'd see their children being baptized that they'd dash on in the water too, and somebody would have to catch them and pull them out. They used to sing: "I'm Going to Drink the Healing Water" and "Jordan's Stream is Cold and Chilly"; and when they sang those songs, somebody would be sure to dive off in the water.

When I was baptized there was a hundred and five or six of us. The preacher was preaching all the time we were marching down to the water. Then he went out in the water in his sock feet, and he went to where the stick was. His helper went with him, because two candidates would always go in the water together. Water just keeps you bouncing, and the helper would hold you and steady you in the water because they sure didn't want your legs to show. When my turn come, the preacher ducked me in the water and said: "I baptize you in the name of the Father, the Son, and the Holy Ghost." Everybody sang a verse of a hymn after each one was baptized, and somebody would throw you a coat. When I come up out of the water, they sang a verse of "I've Found a Friend." The helper put my coat around me, and Momma and others was at the edge to greet me and help me out. They didn't care how wet you got them.

We went back to where we undressed, and got our clothes back on. You were supposed to have a new dress to put on. Then all of us what had been baptized had to walk plumb back to the church, and I know it was as far as from Bell Street to the terminal station. By the time we got back to church it was time for night service, and we attended. They fellowshipped us into the church. We went right down to the front and set right on that bench. We had prayer meeting first. Then we got in a line up at the front to be fellowshipped. All the preachers from any other churches that was there and every last member of the church would come and shake hands with you.

* * *

All us Cartwrights took to religion—excusing Emma. I reckon Sister was sure the devil's handiwork. Oh, she went to church all right, but she was evil. She had a good head on her, and she was real good at church work; she used to be in all kinds of plays. She was stylish too. She was tall, but small-boned and little. I know she never weighed more than 112 pounds dripping wet, and she had very small feet—she wore a three shoe. She could just put on anything and look good. She had tiny little hands, and her nose was so keen and narrow she could wear glasses without shanks or a chain. She didn't have as good hair as the rest of us—hers was reddish and nappy. But when she put all those switches and plaits up there she looked better than anybody else, because she really knew how to fix it.

The trouble with Emma was she was high-strung and high-stepping. She was high-tempered too; she'd get mad just at the pop of your finger. She was just natural-born smarty and mean. Lord, she'd talk hateful! And she'd never take none of it back. Sometimes she and Poppa would have it round and round—and she did provoke him. Sometimes he'd get so mad he'd tell her he'd beat her to death, but it didn't scare her none. She'd say: "Well, it won't do you no good. If you kill me, you can't eat me!" And she didn't take *nothing* back.

How Emma met her first husband, his mother, Aunt Caroline, was old and sick and couldn't write. She would get Sister to write letters to Doug; he was in New York.

When letters came, she'd call Sister to read them to her. Doug wanted to know who was that writing such a nice handwriting for Aunt Caroline. She said: "Tell him your name, Emma." Sister did, and then Doug said for Sister to write him a letter for herself and he'd send her one of his pictures.

I remember when the picture came. Emma was at work, but I just tore it open. Then I ran all the way to the house where Sister was working at, to show her the picture. She whipped me all the way home for opening it.

Then she got Momma to make her a dress to have her picture made. Doug's was so pretty, and she wanted hers to look as good as his. Doug was a light brown-skinned fellow and had coal-black pretty hair, and his eyes sparkled like diamonds. Momma made Sister a blue polka-dot dress with ruffles on the shoulders, and she had the picture made. Doug wrote her that she just suited him right down, and he couldn't wait for summer so he could come home and see his mother and his expected wife.

After that, he got right slack about writing his mother. He'd just write Sister and say what to tell her. Then he come on down. He brought a trunkful of clothes, and he was the most stylish colored man what ever hit Carrollton. He'd change clothes every day, and Sister wore all Baby's clothes as well as her own so she could keep up with him. Baby's dresses were too big for Sister; but she'd pin them up on her and go on, and she'd still look better than anybody else.

Doug stayed a week, and they got engaged. It was getting into cool weather when he came back to live; and little or no time after that, they got married.

They bought a two-room shotgun house. It was one room right behind the other, and the house didn't have no elbow in it. Folks used to say you could stand in front of a house like that and shoot clear through it. Not many people had elbows in their houses though, so Sister didn't mind that. What she really objected to, their house had the planks going straight up and down instead of across like most houses. Doug bought some chicken wire and made a big backyard, and Momma gave them some chickens. They had a nice well.

Doug went on doing barber work in Carrollton, same as he had in New York. But soon he went to feeling poorly, and the doctor told him his work wasn't healthy and to change jobs. He went to a grocery store, but he didn't get any better. Then all at once he just come completely down and got real sick. Sister took over everything then. She was a fine cook and had worked for real wealthy folks in Carrollton, and she went to cooking out again.

While Sister was out cooking, Doug's people would be coming there trying to get him to change his insurance from her name back to his mother's. He had lots of insurance, and he did change it back to his mother. Sister got hold of what he had did, and she come to our house one night late with all her clothes, and she said she had left

Doug. Momma said: "You ain't going to leave that sick man over there by himself." And Momma made her go back.

It rained so hard one day that the water covered their steps. Sister had gave Doug a real hard job to do—she was always hateful to him after she found out about the policies—something like scrubbing the floor or some job she knew he wasn't strong enough to do. When she come home that evening, she said: "I see you didn't do what I told you to." He said: "I was so sick I couldn't." Sister said: "Well, I ain't going to wait on you no more." And with that she picked him up—he had TB and he was just skin and bones—just picked him up like a baby and set him down outdoors by the steps, right in the water.

A neighbor woman got him up, and then his mother and his brother Jed come over and took him with them. He was wet as water and muddy and just a-trembling, and in a bad shape. Late that night they come to our house to get Sister. Doug wasn't even able to get up and down enough to go to the toilet, and he didn't want nobody but Sister to help him. She said she wouldn't go, but Poppa grabbed her up and said: "You go or I'll kill you!" Poppa never really hurt a one of us, but I know for sure he'd have knocked Emma stemwinding if she hadn't gone. She knew it too, and off she went.

Next day she wouldn't even stay off her job though, and some time during that day Doug died. Jed had it in for Sister from then on.

(39)

Sister went to the funeral, but she wouldn't wear mourning and she wouldn't go with the family. She went to a livery stable and told the man she wanted the fastest horse he had and a rubber-tired buggy. He rented her the liveliest slick horse with a red ribbon in his mane. Sister put on a black skirt and a red satin waist and drove to the funeral by herself. On the way to the cemetery, everybody was driving along slow, and here come Sister in the rubber-tired buggy all by herself. She dashed past everybody, and when they got to the cemetery she was already there. It was mortifying.

Almost right then she went to going back with Virgil Keel, her first boyfriend, and she was a disgrace the way she talked about Doug. We was all ashamed of her. She didn't get his policies, but she did get his lodge money from the Knights of Pythias. Soon as she got the lodge money, she went on to Tallapoosa and married Virgil.

Momma never did feel the same toward Sister after the way she treated poor Doug. She really just the same as killed him, and Momma always believed in taking care of sick folks.

Momma was a great hand to nurse the sick and shroud the dead too. Anybody'd be sick, she'd get her lantern and go, any time of day or night. It was my job every night to see was there any oil in that lamp. Momma had a little black velvet shoulder cape, and a little basket with all different kinds of medicine in it. If it was a long ways off and if it was night, she'd wake up my poppa or my brother;

mostly she'd make Little Buddy go with her. If it was near, she'd take me.

We didn't know nothing about no undertakers then; and if anybody died, they sent for Momma. Her and two other women were the shrouding women. Dead folks is so heavy, it would take three women to do it. I went with them many a night. They'd have a kettle of hot water. Anybody had a tin tub then was a big shot; the biggest portion of folks had wooden lard tubs. They mostly had Octagon soap; but if they had a bar of sweet soap, that would be the talk for all the next week. Momma and the other two women would bathe the corpse. If the ironing-board was very narrow, they'd go to the barn and take a door off and lay it on two chairs. They'd put a quilt on it and a sheet—everybody used to keep the prettiest white sheets just especially for that—and then lay the dead on there, and another sheet to cover him up. They'd close the mouth by tying a clean white rag under the chin, and lay a dime on each one of the eyes.

What broke me up from going with Momma to set up with the dead was what Mrs. West did. Because this dead woman had a tin tub—and a tin tub was wonderful, it was so light and easy to handle—Mrs. West wanted to stand her up in the tub to bathe her. She always was bossy. They argued and argued with her, but finally they give in. The dead woman was big, but Mrs. West said they could handle her. So they got the woman in the tub, and then she made some kind of curious noises. They all turned her loose and she hit the floor—the body went one way and the water went the other way. We nearly killed ourselves running that night. Everybody in the house run. Me and Momma went on home. It was just gas or air in the dead woman that made that noise, but it scared Mrs. West and she ran, and that scared us, so we all ran. Then we felt silly, and that made Momma mad. She said she wasn't going to do no more shrouding with Mrs. West. She didn't, either. After that she only shrouded little babies, that she could do by herself.

She quit doing all that after Jeanette was born, though. Momma was deathly sick before Jeanette come, and she just wasn't no good afterwards. Momma didn't have a doctor, but just a midwife. After that, she was sick, sick, sick all the time. Some days she'd nearly die.

Then a friend that lived just below Carrollton asked Momma to come to visit her for a week or two, thinking she'd get a doctor and hoping Momma would get better. So Momma packed a market basket and got ready to go all at once, just before Christmas-time. Jeanette wasn't a year old then. Nobody ever heard of suitcases then. You packed in a market basket and put a towel over it under the handles, and the towel's fringes hung over outside. If you didn't have fringes hanging out, you wasn't nobody.

Momma packed two baskets tight full and got on the train. After she got on the train, she met her younger brother. He saw how sick she was and asked her why she was on the train in that shape. He said: "I know Walt's out of town on a job and doesn't know you're traveling when you're so sick." Momma told him she was going to Grangeville to get well.

I was thirteen then. When Poppa come home and she was gone, he said: "Well, there'll be mighty little Santa Claus this year, with your momma sick and me so busy." He was only home for a day or two, but we got a letter from Momma while he was there. She said for him to come and bring Florrie. She was crazy about Florrie. Florrie was three then. Jeanette was just an arm-baby, and I used to quiet her with butter and sugar in a rag—sugar tits, we called them.

So Poppa packed him a basket, and he and Florrie got on the train. Then we got a letter from Poppa, saying Momma was doing well and he'd write us when she was well enough to come home. We kept a-looking for the letter, but he came on back with Florrie without writing any more.

We kept asking where was Momma, and he said she wasn't doing well at all and he'd brought Florrie back because he couldn't take care of them both on the train at once. He said: "I'm going back tomorrow and get Jennie."

He left the next day for Grangeville again. Momma had two sisters living in Newnan, and they both knew Poppa was going to bring her through there, so both of them came to the depot and saw her. Poppa and Momma had to leave that depot and go to another one to get the train for Carrollton. Momma stepped up in the hack all right, but when they got to the other depot she couldn't get out. The driver drove up to a stob and tied the horse, but Momma didn't make a move to get out or say a word. She just kept looking at Poppa, and she did kind of smile, he said later, but she didn't say anything.

Poppa asked the man to help him get Momma out of the buggy, and they carried her into the waiting-room. She stayed there while Poppa went out to the buggy to get their baskets. While he was doing that, the driver went to the ticket agent and said: "Ain't no need of that man buying two tickets. His wife's dead."

It sure did get away with Poppa. He knew Momma had got worse, but to have her die like that was awful. To make it worse, the ticket agent told Poppa he'd have to get her in a coffin, ready for burial, before he could put her on the train. Momma's sisters said for Poppa to get a wagon and take Momma out to their house, four or five miles in the country. But the ticket agent—and he was quite naturally a white man—said there wasn't no need to take Momma way out in the country. He said: "My woman lives right across from the station here, and she's just as nice and friendly a person as there is. I'm sure she'll let you lay your wife out at her house until you can make arrangements."

Naturally Poppa expected to see a white woman after the man had talked like that; but when he saw her, she was colored. Poppa was so outdone he didn't know what to do. Of course he knew people slipped and did things like that, but this ticket agent had just come right out and told it. Poppa was real mad about it, but he was all tore up about Momma, and away from home, and so upset he couldn't think, so he stayed there.

That ticket agent sure was nice to Poppa though, and so was the woman. They sat up all night with Momma, and the woman even came up on the train with Momma and Poppa the next day. She was dressed to kill. She was the first woman I ever saw with a black silk dress on.

We thought Momma was coming home to get well, and we had supper ready for her. We had everything she liked —red onions, streak o' lean, and a hoecake of cornbread. Every time I think of those things, I just don't want to eat them.

In a small place like Carrollton was then, you'd be known by everybody, white and colored, and word got around that Momma was dead just right away. People all came and they brought us all sorts of things they thought we'd need. They were nice to us because everybody was crazy about Momma. Miss Nell was dead then, but Mr. Gruber came over, and he sat and talked to us a long time. He told Poppa not to worry about getting people to the cemetery, that he'd get a way for everybody to go.

Momma belonged to the Courts of Colanthians, and that order came to the funeral wearing their red aprons and other regalia. All the folks gathered at our house, and two-horse buggies was around the house as far as you could see. Mr. Gruber had called up all the rich white folks and borrowed their rubber-tired surreys to take Momma's friends to the cemetery. Everybody said that was the first colored person's funeral they'd ever seen with the people all going to the cemetery in rubber-tired surreys.

We didn't want to stay in Carrollton by ourselves after Momma died. Poppa was off on jobs a lot, and courting Miss Rachel and coming in late when he was home. Sister begged him to let us move to Tallapoosa and be with her, and he finally did. Houses were plentiful, and Sister got us a nice big one right next door to her and Virgil. Poppa let myself, Baby, Florrie, and Jeanette go. Baby was eighteen or nineteen then, and she kept house for us.

Poppa and both Lee and Buddy stayed in Carrollton. Poppa was in Carrollton maybe as much as a year after we went to Tallapoosa, but it wasn't no time after Momma died that Miss Rachel grabbed him. To make it worse, she bragged about it. Before they were married, he used to bring her over to Tallapoosa when he'd come to see us. She'd act sweet as pie—always bring us something, get up soon and fix everybody's breakfast, tell us names of different flowers and birds and all—but that was just baiting us in till she could get him, and we knew it all the time. None of us ever did have no use for her.

We figured he was going to marry her, and me and the

younger ones sure raised sand. We told him we didn't want no stepmother, and especially not Miss Rachel. Poppa said if he married her she'd be good to us, and Momma was dead and we couldn't have her back, and all such as that, trying to make us happy about what he had in mind. He was betwixt two feelings: he wanted to marry Miss Rachel, and he wanted us to be happy. But, same as Sister said, there's people in hell wanting iced water.

Poppa went with Miss Rachel for just a little while, and then all at once he hopped up and married her. We wouldn't have gone to the wedding if they'd had one, but they didn't have any regular wedding—they was married at the Court House in Carrollton.

After they was married, Poppa come on to Tallapoosa by himself and told us about it. I like to have died. Didn't none of us take it well, we all got upset, but I was more upset than any of them. Babe was old enough to get married herself, and Florrie and Jeanette weren't old enough to realize what it was all about, but I was just the size that really knowed. I was going on fourteen or something like that.

It hit Babe mighty hard too, though. Usually Baby was the last person in the world to talk back. She was really too good to live. She never got mad, and no matter what anybody said to her she'd never argue back. And if you'd say too much, she'd go off and sit down and cry; she just couldn't stand it. She was more like Momma than any of the rest of us. She had ways like Momma, but she was softer. Baby couldn't stand to hear anybody else fussing, much less fuss herself. If any of us others was fighting, or Poppa didn't come home on time, or any little thing like that, she'd go out behind the house and cry just like somebody had whipped her. She had a good suit of long, coal-black hair. I remember patting her on that pretty head and telling her not to cry, lots of times.

All together, I bet Baby never told anybody off more than once or twice in her whole life. But when Poppa married Miss Rachel, she sure spoke her piece. She said to Poppa: "Well, I ain't going to live with no stepmother. I'll get married myself." And blest if she didn't up and marry Fred Sullivan. Right then.

She'd been going with Fred, but I don't know whether or no she was engaged to him. But I don't think she was about to marry him, not so soon anyhow, before Poppa married Miss Rachel. It sure didn't make me feel no better about Poppa and Miss Rachel to have Babe get married right after them. Fred was a duded-up city slick if I ever saw one, and I wasn't noways particular about him. Babe really was crazy about him though, and, to give the devil his due, he was fun.

Poppa and Miss Rachel lived in Carrollton, but we stayed on in Tallapoosa. Lee and Buddy could make it in Carrollton all right whether Poppa had married again or no. They was both old enough and, besides, they'd both been working for a right smart while. Buddy still delivered for the grocery store, and Lee had a job working for the express company.

I remember when Poppa quit farming and Lee first went to working out. First job he had, he went to work at some little store in Carrollton. Looked like to me it was dry goods and groceries and everything together. Lee was a good worker. He had a light foot on the dance floor and he was a sporty dresser, just crazy about his blue serge suits and his white flannel pants, but he was a steady boy too, and he'd make friends easy. He stayed at that store a long time and made himself a good record.

He delivered so much to the Fields's house till Mr. Fields come to like him and told him he'd help get him a job at the express company. I remember plain as broad open daylight, long before Momma died and us girls left Carrollton, every night Lee would be standing backed up to the fire, tall and heavy-built and the spitting image of Poppa, talking about Mr. Fields and going to work at the Express. And then sure enough he did. First he worked in the building and didn't have to go outdoors. Later he got up high enough that he was driving the Southern Express wagon when he got killed.

A mob crowd killed him when he was twenty-one. Three white men and two colored men killed him about a colored woman. Her name was Eva Williams and she was common as pig tracks. She was real fair skinned, and she went with white men and colored both. One white man had told Lee not to let him catch Lee around her any more. Lee said: "She's more my color than yours. I don't see why I can't go with her, and I will." The white man said if Lee wanted to stay alive he better let Eva alone.

This white man got together with two other white men, and with two colored men that had it in for Lee, and they framed it all up and killed him. He was on his way home one night, coming through the white cemetery. These men were all laying around behind the tombstones, and they caught him and killed him right there.

One of the colored men was Sister's first husband's brother. He quite naturally hated Sister, which she did just as good as kill Doug. But this brother, Jed, wanted to jump on her just like she was a man one day, and Lee took her part. So they had a fight, and Jed had stayed mad with Lee for it. The second colored man was mad at Lee because he kept dancing with his girl at the dance hall. The only trouble with Lee, he wasn't scared of nothing.

A long while later, we come to find out who did it. But then, when it happened, all we knew was what Mr. Fields found and what a white man told in court. This white man lived near the cemetery, and he said he had seen a buggy parked there all afternoon, and then he'd seen these men vanishing in the cemetery. Lee come down the dirt road that went on through the cemetery, and it was about nine o'clock at night. This white man told in court that he heard their voices then, one begging for his life, and that he saw two buggiesful of men take Lee off. He said he looked out his window and saw them tying Lee to one of the buggies. He said he heard one say: "No shooting now. I told you that makes too much noise. Just stick him where it'll kill him."

This man said he didn't go out and help Lee because he was scared. He said he couldn't see who the men were, but he could see there was three white and two colored. It was a bright moonlight night and wasn't nothing to hinder him from seeing. He watched till they drove off with Lee.

Lee was supposed to get to work about eight in the morning, to hitch up to go meet the train. Mr. Fields said he didn't show up that morning, and the horse, old Dan, had been galloping up and down and making curious noises and cutting up. Dan had got out of the barn. Mr. Fields didn't know then how come him to be out, and he went to see what was the matter with Dan. He saw Lee through the barn door, laying flat on his face, and he thought Lee was drunk. He went in and took Lee by the shoulder and turned him over, and the dried blood fell out in little pieces out of his head where they'd stabbed him right between the eyes.

Mr. Fields called the police. The neighbors had commenced to gather around, and one white man that they said later was in the killing said to Mr. Fields: "You ought to keep your mouth out of this. We might just as likely have you to bury too." Mr. Fields didn't pay him no mind.

He said besides being a murderer, whoever framed that up about the pistol in Lee's hand wasn't right bright. What they'd done, they'd brought Lee's body back to town and put him in Mr. Fields's barn. They'd laid him on his face and put a quart bottle with a little whisky in it by him, and put a pistol in his hand—fixing like he was drunk and killed himself. Mr. Fields said any child could look at that place in Lee's head and tell it wasn't no pistol wound. He went on ahead and got whoever did such work as that to saw Lee's head and examine it. There was a deep wound, like from an ice pick, but no bullet.

The police locked up one colored man and one white man, but they wangled and twisted and got out of it. Wasn't nothing ever done about Lee's being killed.

Over a year after that, Jed came down real sick and he sent for Poppa. Poppa was a terrible hand not to want to go, but my stepmother said he ought to, so he finally got another man and they went together. Poppa said Jed wasn't as big as your hand; he had TB just like his brother. When Poppa and this other man got in the room, Jed said: "Uncle Walter, I sure am glad you got here. I've done asked God to forgive me, and now I want you to forgive me before I die."

Poppa said: "What have you did to me?"

And Jed said: "I helped kill Lee."

Poppa said he just turned right around and started out of the room, but Jed called him back. "Please listen, Uncle Walter. Lee was all right. We give him time to pray, and he

said he was sorry he hadn't let that Eva Williams alone."
And then he called the names of the three white men and
the other colored man.

"I was just in the bunch," Jed told Poppa. "I just helped
hold him. It was Mr. Stubbs stabbed him. . . . I didn't
know no better, and I was so mad with Emma, and Lee
had took up for her. . . . We had croker sacks to keep
the blood off the buggies. . . . They went on by Eva's
house, and I went with them. . . . She knowed they were
going to try to get Lee. . . . When she let us in, Mr.
Stubbs said: 'Well, we got rid of him, but I got some of
his blood on me.' "

Poppa said: "Don't tell me no more. I got nothing to say
to you, being as you're dying, but I don't want to listen to
you either." And he started to get up again. But Jed just
kept a-talking.

"I want to tell it all, Uncle Walter," he said. "I want to
get it off me. . . . Lee went to his rest, but that boy sure
have rode me at night. . . . and I ain't going to live much
longer. . . . So Mr. Stubbs said to Eva: 'I got some of his
damn nigger blood on my hand. I'll just wipe it off on
your arm. There. That'll be the last you'll see of Lee
Cartwright.' Eva just laughed, and they all had some liquor and Eva had a drink with them."

Two or three days later, Jed died. Only one of the mob
crowd was still living in Carrollton then, and I don't know
which one it was. Poppa said he didn't feel like trying to
catch him, but he wouldn't stay in Carrollton himself any

longer. He come over to Tallapoosa one night and told us. He said he had done sold everything he had, and my step-mother was already with her family in Atlanta.

I said: "Poppa, what about us? Where we going to live at?" And he said he wanted us to stay on in Tallapoosa until he could get a place for us all in Atlanta. I jumped up and said: "In Atlanta! Where all them streetcars and lights is?" I was so glad I woke up little Florrie and Jeanette right then to tell them. I have learned since not to tell things before they happen. Sometimes when you talk things they don't come to pass, and then people have it to laugh at.

3

It was rooming when we first went to Atlanta,
then the woman moved away and let Poppa have the three-room house on Rawson Street. Besides him and me there was my stepmother, Florrie, Jeanette, and Baby and her husband. We left Buddy in Carrollton a few weeks with some friends of ours. We wasn't worried about him, because he wasn't old enough to be courting and running around. Anyhow, hardly no time after we went to Atlanta, Buddy come on from Carrollton.

The house had a little front porch, and on the side was a long porch that went plumb back to the back of the house. The hydrant was right in the yard at the edge of the porch, and I thought that was the wonderfullest thing —not to have to go outdoors to draw water. I drawed more water than anybody, because I thought it was the finest thing ever was to have water right at you that way.

Me and Florrie and Jeanette slept in the front room; Poppa and Miss Rachel slept in the middle room; Babe and her husband slept in the back room; and Little Buddy slept in the kitchen on a cot. If Florrie or any us wanted a drink of water in the night, we'd have to get a pitcherful ahead of bedtime, because Miss Rachel wouldn't want us to pass through their room.

After we got moved in and straightened out, the children started to school. I carried Florrie and Jeanette to kindergarten up on Fraser Street, about three blocks away. I didn't want to go to school; I wanted to go to work. I saw all the other little girls working, and I wanted to work too. Of course they were working because they had to work, and right then I didn't have to, but I didn't have the mother wit to know it.

So I went to work at a boarding-house, washing dishes after I'd carried Florrie and Jeanette to kindergarten. Our stepmother was so mean, I just hated her; I couldn't stand her. She'd always tell Poppa that I wouldn't come home, that she knew it didn't take me so long to carry the children to kindergarten. One reason I got the job washing dishes was I didn't like to come home. I knew how she'd fuss. She'd just dog at me all the time.

Poppa finally said: "Well, you carry the children and let Willie Mae stay home and clean up." So for one while there she was taking them and I was cleaning up. When she'd get back, the house wouldn't suit her; it wasn't done right. The old hussy. I reckon I ought not to say that about her because she's dead now, but that's what she was.

Poppa would always buy plenty of food on a Saturday

—great big sacks of flour, big bags of meal, a whole ham, big pieces of streak-o'-lean bacon, and butter. He'd try to buy enough on Saturday to be the biggest portion of food for the week, so he wouldn't have to buy no more. He did the grocery shopping himself on Saturday when he got paid off.

I said to him one day coming down the street from the store: "You buy all this food, but me and Florrie and Jeanette don't get any of it. We don't know what it is to get a piece of ham or sausage until Sunday morning when you're there." That's one reason I hated Miss Rachel. I'd have called her a polecat except I really didn't have nothing against polecats. She used to take lots of the food and cook for this other man she was slipping with. She called him her sweetheart. Whenever he'd come tomcatting around she'd make us get out and go somewhere and play, or sometimes she'd go next door—that woman was crooked too—and cook for him there.

That's when the fuss came, when I told Poppa we didn't get no food on account of Miss Rachel's sweetheart. He said he couldn't believe it, but I kept telling him. He said: "Is you telling me the truth?" I crossed my heart and hoped to die, but he just stood there and looked at me. He really couldn't believe it.

So things rocked along, and one Saturday he bought a great big piece of cheese. On about Monday I said to myself: "I'm going to see now where the cheese is." I knew it wasn't in the icebox or the safe, because I had done looked. So I went out on the porch where Miss Rachel was sitting reared back in a chair. She had her long hair down her back, and she was just a-combing it. I never will forget it. She was sitting there with her back turned to me, and I felt like hitting her in the head with a hammer, but I didn't want to get locked up.

So I said: "Miss Rachel?" She didn't say a word. She never would answer me the first time. I kept a-calling her and finally she yelled: "What in the hell do you want?" She'd blaze out that way all the time.

I said: "Can I have piece of that cheese Poppa bought Saturday?" She said: "Did he buy cheese?" I said: "Saturday he bought a great big piece." She said: "Well, he must have lost it, because he hasn't brought it here." I said: "I don't know is he lost it, but I know he bought it and I'm going to ask him." She said: "You better not ask him. If you do, your back is mine tomorrow." She meant she was going to beat me. She never really hit me—she did throw the broom at me once—but she used to wear Florrie and Jeanette out. We always had been scared to tell him what she did. On top of that, we didn't have no chance hardly to tell him. He had a job with some contractors, surveying the ground and digging out for the statue of Henry Grady at Five Points, and he'd have to get up real soon in the mornings. He'd go so soon Miss Rachel never would get up and cook nothing for his breakfast; he'd go by a lunch room and get a cup of coffee on his way to work. And he wouldn't get home till way up in the evening.

When Poppa come home that night, we were all sitting down by the open fire in the front room; people didn't know nothing about no living-rooms then, we sit in the front bedroom. Florrie whispered to me: "You going to ask Poppa about the cheese?" I wanted to ask, and I was scared to ask; so I told Florrie to hush up. But after a while I said to myself: "I know he ain't going to let her kill me." So I went in their room.

She was sitting in a little low cane-bottomed chair, and Poppa was in his rocker. I got right by Poppa and said: "Poppa, didn't you buy some cheese Saturday?"

Miss Rachel said: "All right, big woman. I told you not to ask him, but you thought you'd be safe. I'll whip you right in front of him."

She jumped up and pushed back her chair. She went to snatch me and I grabbed up at her face. Poppa pushed me away from her and said: "Rachel, don't you hit her." She commenced cussing. She could do some of the worst talk you nearly ever heard. She said she was going to leave Poppa. He said that wasn't no reason to leave, just because a child asked about a piece of cheese, which he did buy it.

That got him started and he said: "Where *is* all the food going to?" He said the children weren't getting it, and he wanted to know who was. "These children wouldn't be all the time punching holes in cold biscuits and pouring syrup in if they got anything fit to eat," he told her. She said it was a damn lie we didn't get fed right and she'd pack up and leave.

I was sorry I said anything about it, because they fussed all night long. Way after a while I heard her say: "Thank God you've got to get out of here and go to work early in the morning; and if I don't beat hell out of that heifer then, my name ain't Rachel."

Poppa said: "If you put your hand on any one of them, you'll be sorry. You told Willie Mae her back would be yours; so help me God, if you touch any of those children, your so-and-so's going to be mine."

Poppa never was one to talk rough like Miss Rachel did, but he did this one time because he was so mad. He'd have tore her up if he'd known her to hurt us.

The next morning I went in the kitchen, and I was so glad to see Buddy still buried up in the covers. Miss Rachel wouldn't know he was there; she'd be sure he was gone to work. We had a little No. 7 cook stove, a wood stove, and I went to knocking the ashes out, fixing to make a fire. She hollered from their room: "It won't do you no good to be in there cleaning the stove out. Talking about didn't get no cheese and no ham. Well, you ain't going to get a dern thing this morning but your tail whipped."

Then she came and stood in the door with the strap behind her, and she never looked behind the door to see was my brother in the bed, because he never had been before at that time of day. She said to me: "You hurry up and get that fire made. I'm going to show you something, young lady." I went to wiping the table off. Buddy turned over in the bed behind the door and said: "Who's she talking to, Willie Mae?" Then they went to fussing, and they really had it. She was mad because he was there. He said it was his father's house and he could stay home when he wanted to. She said he just stayed because he knew she was going to "whip them gals' tails."

All the time, Buddy was putting on his clothes and reaching down tying on his shoes. "Miss Rachel," he said, "if you do, Poppa won't know you when he comes home tonight." I was so glad then. She called Buddy a sassy son-of-a-bitch. He said: "I ain't going to cuss back at you. I ain't even going to sass you. But you better not whip them children."

They argued and argued, and finally Miss Rachel come down just as nice as could be. She told us she was just trying to raise my momma's children. Children were always going astray, she said, and she was trying to bring us up good. Buddy said: "Raising is all right, but you ought to give them something to eat, and you got no business talking about beating them." She told him I was lying about the food, but I said no, I wasn't. It sure was terrible, but it finally blowed over.

At the time Miss Rachel and my poppa separated, it was a bad winter, with sleet storms breaking trees down, and he had a bad leg. He was working with an iron pick, digging sewers, and he stuck the pick in the fat part of his leg. It got so bad once we thought we were going to have to take it off. The weather kept on awful, Poppa was down in his leg, and Miss Rachel wouldn't go to work. She said she never had worked out and she wasn't going to.

So I did. This job I had to take was nursing a little boy. This was the first job in my life that I really had to get.

Nursing this little boy, I got a dollar and a half a week. That was a good salary then, with me being so young, and women folks weren't getting much more then anyhow. The job was up on Crew Street, and the lady was in bed sick most of the time. I'd get there in the morning about seven o'clock and wash the dishes up, sweep the floor, bring in the paper and milk, and see after this little boy. He was about four years old, and his name was Robert. Me and him had a good time.

His mother would give us good things to eat, and I'd tell her about how mean my old stepmother had been. She'd usually send me to the store, and I'd bring the groceries back. About the middle of the day she'd get up, and we'd mess around and get a few things done. All during the day, long before twelve o'clock come, she'd be giving me and Robert apples and bananas and such. I liked it there.

I'd get ready to go home about five o'clock, nearly supper-time. She'd go in the kitchen, and whatever we had for dinner she'd take up some of all of it and put it in a little pan. It was a good little white enamel pan with a blue ring around it, and not chipped any place. She'd fix my supper in that pan for me to take home, and she'd tell me to hurry and get there while it was still first dark. I thought I was the biggest woman, going with a pan in my elbow—"toting the crooked arm," folks called it.

That dollar and a half, when the lady would give it to me I'd tie it up and pin it on my dress, I'd be so scared I was going to lose it. I'd bring it home and give it to my poppa. He'd get it changed, and then he'd give me a dime and Florrie and Jeanette a nickel. My brother was making about six dollars a week on a laundry truck, and he'd bring that home. Poppa would give him about fifty cents a week. If Poppa wouldn't be home when I'd bring my money, Miss Rachel would ask me for it, but I'd never give it to her.

That old hussy did Poppa awful when they separated. It was so much snow and sleet that morning I knew I couldn't go to work, because I could tell I could hardly get out the gate.

It was Buddy's job to make the fires every morning, but this day he said to Poppa: "What's the use making a fire in the stove? Who's going to cook? If Little Sister goes to work, she can't. You're not able, and I don't know how. So what's the use making a fire in the kitchen?"

Before Poppa could say anything, Miss Rachel blazed out. "I told you your God damn son didn't recognize me! Now you heard what he said! Counted everybody else and left me out! Well, I'll go! I'll let you and your younguns have this God damn house!" She was slinging chairs around and throwing her clothes on all the time she was talking.

Poppa, crippled up as he was, got his cane and started out the door. I'll be jumped-up if he didn't hobble out and get her a dray to move her things. Instead of him coming back, he went on somewhere, but in thirty minutes' time here come not one dray, but two.

Miss Rachel said: "Well, the dirty son-of-a-bitch! He *wants* me to go!" She was surely outdone, and so she got spiteful. She said she'd fix him, she'd strip the damn house. And she all but did it, too. I didn't mind what all else she was telling the men to haul off, but it like to killed me when she started throwing those pretty cut-glass dishes of Momma's in a tub. I throwed a coat over my head and tore out the front door. The snow and sleet was mighty heavy, but I somehow made it over to Mrs. Blake's. She was the only somebody in that block had a telephone. By the time she called the police and they got there, Miss Rachel had the wagons loaded.

We were watching, and soon here the police come, in their little bitty old Ford cars. They went first to Mrs. Blake's. She come out with them and on across the street to our house. She knew Miss Rachel didn't like her, but she wasn't noways scared of Miss Rachel. Mrs. Blake used to sell beer and whisky, and when Poppa would be having trouble with Miss Rachel he'd go over there and get a shot. Miss Rachel said he was going to see her, which I believe he really was, but it wasn't none of my business—and besides, I liked her so much better than Miss Rachel.

When Mrs. Blake and the policemen come over home, they found me just shouting and hollering down, I was so afraid Miss Rachel would get away with all our stuff. The policemen told me to show them which things were my momma's, and I did. They took the sewing-machine and the best bed and the cut-glass bowls and all off the wagon, and we got everything back but the wash pot.

Miss Rachel sure did rear and pitch; but when the drays pulled off, didn't but one driver have a load. She slammed on her hat and out the gate she went, in her black coat suit and cussing every step of the way.

Mrs. Blake told us to lock the house up, and she carried us on over to her house. She cooked us the best dinner, and me and Florrie and Jeanette stayed there until late in the evening. Then she went on over home with us and carried some kindling. One room was practically empty, and the whole house was torn up. She built us fires and put cover on the beds for us and straightened up the best she could, and then went on home.

Shortly after that, Poppa come. When he come in he was dying a-laughing. He said he was across the street in a neighbor's house the whole time, looking at all of us. He wouldn't come out and come on home until he was dead certain it was all over with.

We stayed there on Rawson Street a couple more months. I called myself keeping house, and I worked out too. I kept house pretty good for fourteen years old. But then our cousins on the West Side told Poppa I was too young to be doing all that, and they got us to move over there with them. Poppa and Buddy slept in the hall on one of those old davenport things that opened up.

When we moved over to Mitchell Street with Cousin Mary, I couldn't keep my job because it was too far to go. I tended to Florrie and Jeanette, kept them clean and carried them to school every day, and I cooked for us and cleaned up our part of the house and did all our washing.

Soon after we moved, Poppa's leg got well. He got a big job where they were digging some more sewers, and Miss Rachel would go up there on pay day and try to get his money from him. When Poppa finished up that job, he came home one Saturday with a round hat box. We all run to meet him, the way we did. He went in the house with me hanging on his arm and little Florrie and Jeanette on his pants legs. He hugged and kissed them and pulled my plait. Then he showed us his new hat. He was crazy about a black Stetson hat, and he looked good in them, too.

He had got back to taking us to the grocery store with him, like he did before he married Miss Rachel. So we all went with him to buy groceries, and he bought so much the man had to send them home, it was too much for Poppa to carry. But he didn't tell us nothing.

When Baby come home that night, he picked up our feet and looked at them on the bottom. He said: "You kids get ready. I'm going to take you out on Peters Street and get you some shoes." I was nearly having a fit then, but we still didn't know nothing.

My big sister couldn't understand about all this buying either. Then Poppa said: "I bought all this for a reason. Here's what's on my mind and what I'm going to do." He said: "I'm leaving here tonight at eleven. I'm going to Louisville, Kentucky, and I've done bought me a ticket. That damn Rachel is about to run me crazy—on my job every day, picking at me, trying to get my money, and making threats on my life—and I'm leaving here. I've bought plenty of food to last you a couple of weeks and I'll send money until I find a place for us to live."

He give Babe some money and Cousin Mary two months' rent. She didn't charge us but a dollar and a half a month for our part of the house. Then he give me the first dollar he ever did, and Florrie and Jeanette fifty cents. He called Buddy out and talked to him and give him some money too.

Near train-time Buddy and Fred and my cousin's husband went to the depot with Poppa. Before they'd been gone thirty minutes, Miss Rachel rolled up in a hack, dressed to kill, the old big-busted thing, and a hat cocked on one side of her head. This was a Saturday night, and she knew Poppa would have his pay.

Cousin Mary throwed her off the track by telling her Poppa had done been gone since six o'clock. "He must be half way to Birmingham by now," she said. I thought Miss Rachel would have a fit and fall in it. She went to screaming and carrying on, and I got right nasty my own self. It wasn't nice, but I was only a child and I could have snatched her bald-headed. She said she'd jerk a knot on me.

We was all carrying on something awful when Baby settled the whole thing. Baby wouldn't even know how to talk ugly, but she sure read Miss Rachel's title clear. She went to the porch and said, just as nice and quiet: "Miss Rachel, we just got enough of you. Poppa's gone, and you can't get him, and you're not going to touch Willie Mae. Furthermore, just get on off this porch and out of this yard. We're through with you." All us others hushed our mouths and stood around and listened—which it was something to pay heed to when Baby spoke up about anything—and then Miss Rachel threw her rump up on her shoulder and went on and got back in the hack and left.

About Tuesday a special-delivery letter come from Poppa, and he wrote it to me. He said he was going on a job real soon and would get us up there quick as he could. He sent us money to get some clothes, because he said the little girls in Louisville sure did dress up. He said houses were plentiful, and wasn't no worry about finding a house soon.

Fred worked at a dress factory, and he told us to come out there one night and get somebody to fit us up with dresses, because he could get them there cheaper than we could in a store. One I got was heavy white Indianhead, boxpleated all the way around the skirt, and a square neck.

Another one was blue checked, gathered all around. I got a pink candy-stripe one too, and a solid blue. We got the little girls dresses downtown; they didn't have any children's sizes at the factory.

I don't know how long it was, but one day here come two tickets for Fred and Buddy, and they like to have had running fits about going to Louisville. Buddy didn't go to bed at all that night. They went on, and I hated to see my brother go, but we got on all right. I saved my new dresses for Louisville. I wouldn't even put them on, but I nearly wore them out showing them to people.

I got me a job in a laundry, and I was the smallest somebody there. Miss Mabel, the boss lady, said to my cousin what took me there: "What did you bring that baby here for?" That scared me, because I just knowed then I wouldn't get a job. Cousin Ida told her about Poppa being in Louisville, and Miss Mabel said: "I don't care. She's too young. What can she do here? We don't need no sweeper. We don't need no water boy. What could we put her to doing?"

My cousin said: "Well, she could shake linen." Miss Mabel took me on and put me to shaking. She talked snappy, but she didn't mean no harm. Some of the women working there got mad when she hired me. They said I was keeping a grown woman out of a job and getting paid three-fifty a week just like a grown person. So some of them were real mean and made it hard for me.

The biggest portion of them were kind to me though,

and they got on those women that were treating me so bad. Cousin Ida especially. She said: "This is my brother's child, and I'll whip you all one by one if you lay a finger on her." After that I got to be the pet around there. They called me "the baby," which of course I was the youngest thing at the laundry.

I was a shaker all the time I was there. Laundries then washed everybody's clothes together. They'd be separated in net bags, but all the bags were washed in the same place together in a great big washer. Then they'd wring them out in a wringer, but there wasn't nothing like a drier. The men would push them in trucks to the tables, and they'd pile up as high as the window. The more lots you shook out, the more money you made that day.

I worked at the laundry until Poppa sent for us to come to Louisville. I don't know how long it was, but it was long enough that I bought myself plenty of underclothes, shoes and socks, some dresses and things for Florrie and Jeanette, and I had five dollars in money. When I left the laundry, everybody there, white and colored, brought me packages for go-away presents—handkerchiefs, socks, soap, powder, ten-cent rings and barettes, and one brought me a red-collar middy blouse.

I went on home that Saturday evening, and we got all finished packing. My sister had a suitcase. She'd been living in Atlanta for a while and had got up high enough to have a suitcase. The neighbors brought us different things for our lunch on the train, and Baby put everything in a willow basket with a top that closed.

We went down to the terminal station Monday morning—me, Florrie and Jeanette, and Baby. Florrie and Jeanette were just little old girls, and they wouldn't go without their little red chairs. Besides that, Florrie had her teddy bear and Jeanette took her doll. I carried the food. We were sitting in the station with all this stuff when the man come in calling the trains. When he hollered, "Louisville," Lord bless my soul, up we put. I left the basket of food in the waiting-room, Florrie and Jeanette forgot their chairs, and we all sprung up and tore right on out to the gate.

We nearly starved on the train, because we'd been so excited about the trip that we hadn't hardly eaten for two days. We stopped at Lexington, Kentucky, and we was growl hungry, but we couldn't get anything to eat. They didn't allow colored folks to get off the train at Lexington. Some of the colored folks on the train even kept the shades drawn when we went through there, so none of those white folks would see us. So we just didn't have a bite to eat, because we were scared to try to get out and buy something. And when we got to Louisville that night about twelve o'clock, we all had the hungry headache.

4

When we got to Louisville the snow was so
deep it was up to my knees. I'd seen snow, but nothing
ever like that before. Snow had blown and banked up
against the sides of the houses, and men were going around
with snowplows. I just looked and looked. Folks said that
was the worst snow had been there for years.

Poppa laid off from work that day to be with us. He
had got a job as a blower at the biggest foundry in Louisville. That white slick stuff sinks and bathtubs are made
out of, Poppa's job was to finish it off. He used to wear
some sort of muzzle when he worked on it. I guess he was
using something so strong it would have eat him up without it.

My cousin had a three-room house. I don't know how
in the name of the Lord she did it, but she kept us packed
up in there with her for about three weeks until the
weather opened up and we could find us a house. Poppa
put us all out to looking, and before long we found a nice
six- or seven-room house. Me and Florrie and Jeanette

slept in a room together, Poppa and Buddy had a room together, and Babe and Fred was in the third bedroom.

There was money supposed to be buried in the coal house in the backyard. Some days I'd go out there and there'd be the curiousest whining and terrible noises in the coal house. That's one reason we could get the place. Nobody else would live there; they was scared. Every day, some time way up in the day, it never missed, two birds would dart in the front door or the back door and zip right to the mantelpiece. We'd take a broom and try to run them out without hurting them, but it didn't do a bit more good than if I tried to chase the smoothing-iron out of the room. It was some kind of a sign, I reckon.

People in Louisville, white and colored, would go and hunt money just like people here in Atlanta now go downtown and hunt a sale. I had seen folks before digging for money, but up there they were bad about it. Every Sunday, or any day they wasn't working, you could see crowds of people out with their money rods, looking for money. We knew about ten or twelve people what found money that way. My cousin Tom found some once.

Somebody was always telling Poppa about what others had found, so he got interested in it and he sent off for a money rod. It has a big wheel and a little bitty wheel, with a chain hitched around them both. Then there's a long something with a sharp point going down toward the ground. If there's money somewhere, the two wheels go to whirring.

Poppa was bound to find it if there really was any money in the coal house. He went out there one morning after he got his rod, and he dug until evening. He said when he struck the pot he broke it. It was a great big black iron pot. Wasn't no paper money in it at all; it was all silver and gold. It was American money, just like you could spend now. And some old watches, and one big silver pitcher. There was a stack of papers too, but they had been there so long they had done rotted.

There were about five men digging with Poppa, because he had to have some help, and they fixed up ahead of time how much each one would get if they found money. Poppa got the biggest portion. He was always going to be the boss of things, and after all it was his house where he rented at, and he was the one who got the rod to look there. I don't know how much he got, but he went and paid down on the prettiest home we'd ever seen, and he gave Buddy money to make a trip back to Atlanta and Carrollton to visit, and he bought me and the little girls clothes, and he still had some money to put up.

About a month or two after Poppa found the money, we moved to the new house. It was around on 12th Street, and it was a beautiful place. It was a slate-blue house, trimmed with white borders, with a porch going all the way around. The back porch was latticed. I used to get out there on that latticed back porch, and nobody could have told me I wasn't rich as cream. There was the prettiest sink in the kitchen, a big pretty bathtub—the first bathtub we'd ever had—and a little lavatory near the back door.

The house had a half-story too, and we used that part for a trunk room. And it was high enough off the ground that the little girls could play under there. I believe the house cost $1,300. It had a white picket fence all the way around, and shade trees scattered about in the front yard. The backyard had a peach tree and a grape arbor.

That was the first time I ever had a room to myself. It was a small little room, but it was cute. I had a nice little half-iron bed painted with some kind of golden bronze paint, and a white dresser and a white chair. Babe bought them at a secondhanded store. Poppa let her fix the house like she wanted it, and she really could fix a nice-looking house.

As swell as our house was, we didn't have drinking water in the yard. Downtown at a square was a big pump. It was the best and the coldest water I ever put in my mouth; in the summer you didn't have to use no ice to cool it. We'd have to go three blocks to get this water to drink and cook with. The water we used to clean with, we got in the backyard. That water had a green look to it, and we'd have to let it set all night; then it would be clear. If you used it without setting, it would ruin your clothes.

It was hard to get used to going three blocks after drinking water, because, no matter how bad a house was in

Carrollton or Atlanta, your drinking water was right there. We had special water buckets with tops and pretty dippers. Poppa told me not to go up to the square by myself ever at night after water, because boys used to hang around the pump there just like they hang around places in other towns. I didn't want to go anyhow.

Being unhandy about the water was the only thing wrong about that house, though. Poppa was really crazy about it, and he always wanted grass in the yard. Every evening he'd come home with ten or fifteen cents worth of grass seed and sprinkle it around. When we left from there, after Poppa died, the yard was covered with green grass.

Buddy was so excited about his trip to Georgia that he was crazy as a Betsy bug, and a Betsy bug is the foolishest thing there is. He bought a little straw hat, tight as beeswax, with a checkedy band all the way around it. He was trying on that hat all night before he left.

When he went back down to Georgia and shot off his mouth about how well Poppa was doing, that stirred Miss Rachel up. That's what started her to writing up there to try to make Poppa take her back. She seed he was doing so well, so quite naturally she wanted to come back to him. She said she saw Poppa was doing well from all those Dolly Varden suits Buddy had. I don't know what she meant, but that's what she called them.

Poppa didn't get over one or two of her letters, because

we just met the postman and took them. It upset us some when we saw Poppa reading that first one or two, and after that we just took them as fast as the postman would bring them. When Poppa read the first ones he 'lowed: "I *told* that boy not to go down there blabbing his head off." But he looked to us like he might be pleased to take her back, and that scared us.

I'd put the letters in the stove when I got them. Babe would always ask if we tore the letters up. I'd say: "No need to tear them up and burn them too." Sometimes I'd read them; other times I wouldn't have a chance. If I'd see Poppa coming, I wouldn't have time to read them; I'd just stick them in the stove and be stirring up the fire when he came in.

Miss Rachel would carry on a lot of foolishness in those letters. She'd say she'd forgive Poppa if he'd forgive her, and beg to come back, and all such as that. She wanted to see Louisville, I know, and she wanted him back too because he really was nice to her and crazy about her before she got so mean to us. If Poppa had just married Miss Flora—he went with her some after Momma died—we never would have objected. He knew how we liked Miss Flora and couldn't stand that old heifer, but he used to tell us we couldn't pick no wife for him.

Poppa didn't find out we were taking his letters for over a year. He was sitting across the street one day talking to another man, and here come the postman to our house. He seen Florrie and Jeanette run under the house with a letter.

They was small, but they could always tell when it was a letter from Miss Rachel. I don't know could they tell the handwriting or what, but they could always tell; and if I was at school or some place they'd dart under the house with it and hide it there. We didn't know that, any of us, until this day Poppa seen them. He come on across the street and said: "Where's that letter you went under the house with?" Both of them went to crying, and then Jeanette went to putting it all on Florrie.

Poppa broke a switch and told Florrie to go under the house and get the letter. She said: "You want me to bring them all?" He said: "What 'all'? Is there more?" Came to be that lots of times when they'd hid letters under there they'd got to playing and forgot them, and there was a lot of them under there. She went and brought them out, and they was all wet and moldy. Once on Poppa's birthday Miss Rachel had sent him a letter with ten dollars in it and said for him to buy him a silk shirt. The ten-dollar bill was all moldy too, but Poppa turned it in and got a new one.

He switched both Florrie and Jeanette and when Babe come home he got after her about it. Florrie and Jeanette had told him Babe told them to hide the letters. Babe just up and told him: "We didn't want you to take Miss Rachel back." But she denied it about telling the children to put the letters under the house, which she really had done it; she didn't realize they'd be so forgetful and let them pile up under there. Poppa told Babe he wasn't going to take Miss Rachel back, he had done made up his mind and got settled, but he sure lit into the whole shooting match of us about stealing mail.

That broke it up from mail being under the house, but it didn't break us up from burning. He didn't get none of the letters that came from her. After that happened we did always tear them open to see did they have any money in them, but they never did any more.

I went to the 12th Street School. It was three or four stories high, and it was the best and stoutest school building I'd ever been in in my life. I couldn't get my lessons when I first went there for looking at the schoolhouse. It really was beautiful.

The children there wore more ribbon on their hair than I ever saw. In Atlanta they wore ribbon, but not as much as in Louisville. There they wore more ribbon and they wore it prettier. Babe told me to see how they fixed it and she'd get me some.

I asked one little girl and she told me where to buy the things—it was at some five-and-ten—and she showed me how her ribbons was fixed. She said: "If I had hair as long and thick as yours, I'd just wear it up on top of my head and tie a big bow up there, like my big sister." Which of course I couldn't do that; her big sister was a grown young lady and I was just a child.

The combs had holes in them and you'd run the ribbon through the holes and tie a bow with the ends. They called them tuck combs. A tuck comb fit around the back of your head like a cap and they'd have two rosettes on the sides or either the ends tied in bows. Babe went to town and bought me some tuck combs and two or three kinds of ribbon. After that, when I'd see any of my little girl company coming to the house, I'd take out all my combs and all my ribbons and lay them out on the dresser—I was so scared they wasn't going to see them.

There was one little girl I couldn't stand to save my life. She wanted all us other children to mind her and always do as she wanted to. Her father and mother were big shots. They were in the undertaking business, so they were quite wealthy. They had big cars and a beautiful big home and everything you could think of. This little girl could change clothes whenever she had a mind to, she had so many. The other children liked to play at her house because she could always have nice things to eat for them, but she had awful nasty ways. She thought she was better than anybody else.

One day she told me: "I don't like you because you're from Georgia." So I went to telling her why all I didn't like her. I said: "You think you got more than anybody else on earth." She put her hands on her hips and said: "Well, I *have* got more than anybody else around here!" I said: "You haven't got one bit more than my cousin." I wondered where was any cousin of mine had anything; but I had to say something to her, she was so hateful. The other children didn't pay her no mind, but she used to tell them her daddy said I was an old Georgia cracker and not to play with me.

I purely despised her daddy anyway, because I was there when he pulled a real scoundrelly trick on my cousin Iona. Iona had eight-hundred-dollars worth of insurance on her mother and when she died, since they'd been knowing this undertaker a long time, quite naturally he was the one the family called.

He come on, and he told them he was so sorry to hear about their trouble. But he told them their mother was better off to be out of her misery. They put her in the basket and carried her out to the dead wagon. It was a long thing like a willow basket; they don't use them any more.

Then he had to write up something. I don't know whether you call it the death list or what, but it had when she was born and where she was born, and how long she'd been sick, and the doctor who waited on her. Then he wanted to know about her insurance. So Cousin Iona gets the policies out and gives them to him and he looks them over. Then he wanted to see the book. The book's the main thing. He wanted to see was she up in her payments.

Iona said when she went for the book everybody was just as solid and dry as a chip, wasn't a tear to be shedded, by the undertaker nor none of them either. But after he looked over the policies and the book, he went to wiping his eyes.

"Oh, Lord," he sniffled. "Poor Mother. Oh, darling Mother's gone. No more Mother." And crying down all the time. Quite naturally that made Iona go to crying too, and pretty soon the whole family commenced to crying. So the undertaker told them he just couldn't write no more, he was too upset, and for them to come on down to the shop. He was going to get them down to the shop while he had them crying good, and then knock them out.

They couldn't go right then though, he'd made them feel so hurt they couldn't go out. But they went the next day—Iona and Addie and a couple more of them, and they taken me along. Soon as we got there he said: "Well, you all come on in and see Mother. I been in there all morning with our darling Mother, just me and Mother alone." He went to wiping his eyes and started again.

We went on in the room where she was laid out at, and he said: "Just look at her. Now, don't she look sweet? I can just see her sitting up there by The Throne, beautiful Mother." Then he cried some more and said, just like a poem: "Sleep on, Mother, and take your rest. We love you, but God loves you best."

The baby sister, Addie, they just had to carry her back to the car at that. She couldn't stand it. So then the undertaker said: "Now we'll go and see about Mother's things. I've picked out all the things what I want her to have."

He opened the door and we went on in the room where the caskets was. Iona said: "Here's a nice one I'd like to have for Momma." He told her: "No, we can't put darling Mother in that. No, no. I just don't want Mother to be put in that." Then we come to another one that Iona liked, but he went to moaning again—"Oh, darling Mother, sleep on" and all such as that. So we knew he didn't like *that* one.

Anyhow, Iona said: "Well, just tell me how much is this one that I like?" He told her it was two hundred and fifty dollars, but that was too cheap for Mother. Hard as Mother done toiled and worked in this life, he said, and then to be put away in something that cheap—he just couldn't stand to put Mother in that one.

So Iona asked him, and he showed her the one he wanted them to get. He showed us a beautiful gray couch, a great dropside couch. "*This* is what we want to put Mother in," he said. "Now, I can just see Mother laying back in there with that beautiful smile on her face and looking so happy." Then he'd stomp his feet and say: "Won't she, chillun?" And they'd all holler: "Yes, sir. Yes, sir." So then he was satisfied at that, and we went on to look at robes.

Iona said: "But Momma has a beautiful dress that she said she wanted to be buried in." Right then the undertaker started crying down again and wiping his eyes, and he said they just couldn't put Mother on that beautiful couch with an ordinary dress on. "You just put that dress aside," he said. "You'll be glad you kept it to remember darling Mother by."

Then he said: "Now, this is what we'll put on Mother." And it was a beautiful soft gray robe with silver lace let in it. And it was seventy-five dollars. The slip to go with it was some gray kind of silk-looking stuff, and it was twenty-five dollars.

One of the children said: "Do we really have to buy a slip to go with the robe?" The undertaker told them, he said: "Any other slip wouldn't let the robe look right. We have to get the slip to match the robe. When Mother be carried down that aisle, we don't want nothing to look short about Mother. And if she don't have this slip, the robe just won't look right." So they bought the slip too.

Iona said: "We'll come down before the funeral and fix Momma's hair." He told her oh, no, no, he had a woman there who would make her look just like Mother ought to look. So they agreed to that. Which of course every new thing they agreed to, it was costing them that much more.

When it come time to figure on the cars they'd need for the funeral, he told them, he said: "I'll put you down for seven cars. If you don't need them all, you don't have to pay for what you don't use." One of them said: "Oh, we won't need nothing like seven cars, because some of our friends have cars and will use them." He said no, no, no, he didn't want none of those cars in Mother's funeral. He wanted all the cars to go behind Mother to be just alike, and they were all Packards.

They come on out then and went on in the office to sign the papers for the whole bill. He told them, he said: "I know for the last night you all want darling Mother brought back home with you." Iona and them was trying to decide—they didn't know, the place was small, and then too it would be another expense to take her back and forth again. But before they could say no, he started up again.

He said: "Oh, yes, that's just got to be done. We got to bring darling Mother back home." So then he yelled out all at once: "Don't you all want darling Mother back home her last night to be out on earth?" And they all yelled: "Yes, yes! We want our Momma back home!"

He got out one of the Packards and carried them all home, and the next day the funeral was.

All during the funeral he kept standing over the couch saying over and over: "Oh, Mother, you look so sweet," and crying. He had them all boo-hooing again just in a flash. He'd done worked on them so that by the day of the funeral time they'd look at him they'd go to crying. The preacher preached the funeral, and they carried her on to the cemetery with that long line of Packards behind her. When they were letting her down in the ground, the undertaker said: "Good-by, Mother. Good-by, darling Mother. We did all we could for you, Mother."

In the next day or two Iona gets a bill from him and she sees he done mothered her out of the whole eight hundred dollars.

Every day after school I'd change my clothes and do some cooking and washing. I fixed supper practically every night. Babe worked at the tobacco factory, stemming tobacco. You have something on your finger like a thimble, and it strips the leaves off the stem. That factory made plug tobacco, cigarettes, and all kinds of tobacco.

When school was out, all the children—like they do now—would get a job and make some money. The girl next door told me to go with her to the nut factory. I said: "Can you eat any nuts?" She said: "All you want." I asked her how much you made there and she said: "Lots of money. I worked there last year, and some weeks I'd have five or six dollars."

Oh, I wanted to go there too, so I asked Poppa, and he said I could. The boys would crack the nuts and bring them around to us. They wanted the halves to be in solid pieces; all the pieces that were broke went into one aluminum tray, and the whole pieces in another. Then they'd weigh them and the men would figure up how much you made that day, so much by the pound. I thought I was picking out just as many nuts as my friend was, but that first week I made sixty cents. What happened was, I think I ate about ninety dollars worth of nuts and didn't put hardly any in the trays. At home they all fell out laughing about me and the nut factory. Poppa said: "If you ever ask to go back to work at that place, I'll beat you to death." He was laughing too, but I didn't go back.

I went into the mutton-suet factory. I just cold out meant to get me a job some place. I worked there three or four weeks and I did very well, but that odor—I just couldn't stand it. We'd have to take all that sheep fat and stack it, and I couldn't get the odor off my hands no matter how I washed and washed. I made pretty good there, but that odor made me so sick I couldn't eat, so Poppa told me to quit.

Then I went to work at the chewing-gum factory. That was the first job I ever made ten dollars a week, but it was five miles off if it was an inch, and when we'd get off at five in the afternoon it would take me until nine to get home. We might could have got home a little sooner if we could have walked steady as hard as we knew how to go. But we'd be so tired from working all day, we'd stop and rest on people's doorsteps and curbs. So Poppa told me to stop there, and by that time summer was over.

Next year the other children asked me how would I like a vegetable farm. We was used to cotton and corn, not vegetable farms, but I said I'd try it. We'd leave home before day in the morning. We'd get on the railroad track and walk from six to seven miles every morning to those farms. Mostly they'd put us to taking up onion sets with pitch-forks. They'd pay fifteen cents a bushel, and I'd make from two dollars to two-fifty a day. I really liked picking onion sets; it was fun. With a pitchfork, you could dig up three rows at a time; they were planted real close together, and you could just fork them up.

The man kept the baskets in the barn, and each picker could get as many as he wanted. You'd have to watch out for your own baskets though, and be hard and tough about it, or somebody would take yours and you'd have to go all the way back to the barn before you could fork up any more sets. When you had your baskets full, you'd throw up your hand and the man or his son would drive over in the wagon and pick up your baskets full of sets, and then he'd give you chips. Like if I had six basketsful, he'd give me six chips. I'd always have a tobacco sack, and I'd keep my chips in that and pin it on my dress. That's what we all did. The man would empty our baskets and give them back to us, and we'd start forking up onions again. Every day at quitting-time the man would pay you off according to how many chips you turned in.

Most of the time we'd carry our lunch, and at twelve we'd go up to the nearest saloon and sit up to the counter. They'd sell us the best bowl of soup and crackers for ten cents—you could see big pieces of beef in the soup, and all kinds of vegetables. Most of the other children would drink beer. It was a nickel for a big tall mug with a handle on it. I didn't drink any beer, and they used to throw that up to me. They'd say: "She's a Georgia cracker. She drinks water." I didn't care. I liked that job.

Sometimes we used to barrel potatoes and get six cents for every barrel we filled. I've made as high as four dollars or four-fifty a day barreling potatoes and crating roasting-ear corn and tomatoes. Poppa would give me half what I made, and I knew the more I made the more I'd have for myself, and I used to outwork all the other children. They used to play and fool around some, but not me.

The woman next door to us used to take care of Florrie and Jeanette while we was all at work. I told Poppa if I could take them with me to the field, we wouldn't have to be paying nobody to take care of them. He said: "But those children couldn't walk all that distance. You can hardly make it your own self." Well, they couldn't, but I knew there were some colored folks used to have trucks. I went around and gave my name and address to everybody with a truck. I told them I had to take my little sisters with me, and they couldn't walk six miles to the field, and when I couldn't get a ride for them I'd lose a day's work.

About three times a week after that somebody would come by for us soon in the morning. Sometimes they'd be just heard about me from some of the ones I talked to. They'd drive up and stick their heads out and holler: "This where the girl lives what needs a ride for her little sisters?" So then I'd grab up Florrie and Jeanette, and off we'd go to the field.

After I started that, Poppa bought them some overalls and sundown hats, little straw hats, wide with a rubber under the chin. He told me not to work them when the day got up so hot—to let them go to a saloon or under a shade tree. I always did that, and they never had no trouble, little as they were.

Men always paid every day for work such as that. One day me and the little girls together made six dollars and something. Poppa grunted when we give him the money. "Made more than I did today," he said. By the time school opened up in the fall, I'd be done made enough to buy my dresses and shoes and all.

The last Christmas we was in Louisville, that was the Christmas I really had a Christmas. Poppa was going with a woman there, and I noticed she'd come in sometimes and say to him: "You really ought to get it for her, smart as she's been all year." He'd say: "I know, but I can't hardly see that much money go out for something like that." Me and Babe heard them and we wondered what was they talking about and who was it for.

Large as I was, I still thought there was a Santa Claus. Children would tell me there wasn't, but I'd go right back and ask Poppa, and he'd say there was and I'd believe him.

Those girls in Louisville would have the prettiest dolls you ever seen. It was a doll Poppa and this woman was talking about, and it was for me. Children then played with dolls a heap longer than they do now. Poppa went on to the store on Tenth and Magazine and got me the biggest colored doll. It was good and three feet tall, with long black curls and the prettiest blue dress—looked like to me it was a silk dress. I didn't see another girl had a doll like it. And there was a beautiful blue coat for me, with a fur collar, and a big blousy cap that you pulled over and it had a tassel on the side.

Florrie and Jeanette got small dolls and doll carriages. I didn't get but one toy, but that was that wonderful doll, and then I got those nice clothes too. That Christmas morning when I saw that doll, I like to have had a fit. I just jumped for joy. Me and Florrie and Jeanette got right out on the street with our fine Christmas presents, and we knocked them other children off the map.

*   *   *

That woman Poppa used to go with, the one what got him to give me that wonderful doll, was named Paralee Hughes. I'm not sure, but I think he met her on the streetcar going back and forth to work. She was a sporty type of woman, and liked to be always going to parties and shows. Poppa wasn't like that. I bet he didn't go to a show three times in his life before he started going with her. Poppa was a great hand to go to church, and Paralee never did care nothing about going to church. She'd just want to lay around and sleep on Sunday morning, then get up and go out to some of those wide open places where people was drinking and dancing and having a good time. You could go to a beer garden any time of day or night in Louisville then, and that's what she wanted to do. Just get her to a beer garden and let her be sitting up there soaking up beer, and she'd never think about going to church. Poppa wasn't used to that kind of thing, and he said: "I think a lot of Paralee, but I never would marry her." He kept on going with her though. He was going with her when he died.

It came about that some women and men were arguing

at the box factory over something had happened in Atlanta years ago, and they wanted to prove it by Poppa. He was in the saloon and grocery store across the switchyard from the box factory. The saloon was in front and the grocery store in back. When you paid your grocery bill, they'd always give you a bowl of soup either a glass of beer. Poppa had paid up the grocery account and ordered more, and then gone up front to get his beer or soup. He took the beer that evening, and he was setting there drinking it when these folks called him.

This man come in looking for Poppa. He said: "We got up an argument over at the box factory, and I want to see can we prove it by you." Poppa told him he'd come soon as he finished his beer, and the man went back. When Poppa finished his beer he walked out the door and started across the switchyard. I don't know how many tracks was there, but it was always dangerous—you couldn't hardly make it across there. A woman was coming across the yard from one side and Poppa was going across from the other side, and this train tore them both up.

It knocked Poppa a long way, and his head hit on a big rock. All on his left side was tore up, but his right side wasn't hurt at all. It cut the woman up in a thousand pieces, and her black voile skirt with the silk folds was all wound up around the wheels.

Some said the train was on the wrong track, and some said the engineer and fireman both was drunk, but we never knew. We never knew either why couldn't Poppa and that woman hear the train coming. All we knew was it was the train's fault, because the Kentucky Central paid the families. It was a right smart of relatives to pay, too, because that train hit people all up and down the track and killed eight people in one hour that evening.

First thing I knew about it, we heard a woman coming up the street hollering, asking where the Cartwrights lived. Then the woman was beating on the door. Me and Babe was tired, and we was lying down in our petticoats. We both jumped up and run to the door when she went to beating on it. The woman said: "Oh, you all just laying up here resting in your underclothes, and your Poppa done got killed." We said: "Not our Poppa!" But it was.

Babe couldn't get on her clothes, she was so upset. She just grabbed a bathrobe and lit out. She wouldn't let me go with her, so I stayed with Florrie and Jeanette. Almost before I could get the door shut behind Babe, the lawyers went to pouring in, wanting to take the case. One even come in a rolling-chair.

Babe didn't get back until late that night. She had stayed with Poppa until the ambulance come for him and took him to the hospital. He was suffering so bad they wanted to give him something right then to kill him, but Babe wouldn't let them. They put him in the ambulance and she went to the hospital with them. They dressed his wounds, but he was already unconscious by the time they got him to the hospital.

The house was just crawling with them lawyers when

Babe got back home. She told them to go away, and she cleared them out of there just in a hurry. Then she told me she didn't think Poppa would live. She said the whole side of his face was lifted off and you could see his teeth before they put bandages on him.

We went down the next morning to see where he got hit at. I saw a dollar bill sticking up on a stick near the train track, and I saw that woman's black voile skirt all wound round and round in the wheels of the train. I saw other things too, but I still can't stand to think about them. Folks wasn't as swift then to clean up after accidents as they are now.

Soon as they'd let us, we went to see Poppa at the hospital. He'd know us, everybody but me, but he didn't know where he was at, and he'd call for people had been dead a long time. Looked like his mind would just come and go. It was early on a Tuesday evening it happened, and he died the next Wednesday.

My cousin what had lived in Louisville a long time said: "You ain't in Atlanta, you know. You got to serve whisky at a sitting-up in Louisville. Nobody's going to sit up with Uncle Walt unless you let them have some whisky to drink." Fred said: "Well, we'll sit up by ourselves then, because we sure ain't going to do no drinking over Uncle Walt." That was the onliest time I ever knew Fred to show any git-up. Ten or twelve did set up with Poppa, but that wasn't as many as would if we'd had whisky. If we'd have let them have whisky, we wouldn't have had room for how many would have come.

5

After Poppa died, Fred got in a tizzy to go to Adel. His mother had left Virginia when he did and had gone back to South Georgia where she come from, back to Adel. Pretty soon Fred and Buddy went on down there. Fred called himself going down there to set up a pressing-club, but we didn't believe him. He fooled us and did it, but he put it up in Sparks, about two miles from Adel.

Poppa's money did it for him, the insurance money and the railroad money. Fred called himself the guardian of the family after Poppa got killed, and he got the whole push. He got the insurance money, the railroad money, the house money (we sold the house right away; it was too much for us to keep up with Poppa gone), the Knights of Pythias money, and the Odd Fellows money.

Fred said he had come to be the boss of the family, and he handled all the money. I don't know how he fixed it up that way, but he sure did. He called himself the guardian and Babe the administrator, but Babe didn't have no say in any of it. She was so crazy about him that she just let him take everything in charge. Then too, she might have been some scared of him, the way lots of women are of their husbands. And he guardianed us out of every red cent.

We were all supposed to get money from the railroad when we came of age. The railroad paid Poppa's hospital bill, they buried him, and they held back a certain amount of money for each one of us for later, but we never did get any of it. We were so young when it happened, and Fred right quick went to bossing us all around, and then they took us down to Adel, and we never did know how to go about getting our portion of the money.

Anyways, Fred and Buddy went on down to Adel, and we didn't stay in Louisville hardly two months after Poppa died. When he went down there Fred was writing to Babe twice a week, and soon he sent for us. He said he'd found us a nice house in Adel and his mother would stay with us, and it all sounded wonderful. We caught the train and out we put.

We got to Adel at midnight, and wasn't a Lord's soul at the station to meet us and the rain was just pouring down, just a regular gulley washer. We got a hack, but the driver said where we wanted to go certainly was bad. He said you had to go over a creek and the water might be over the bridge, and if he was us he'd rather stay in the waiting-room all night. But Babe wanted to go on, so we did. The bridge had all but washed away, the water come plumb up inside the buggy, and it's a wonder we didn't all get drowned.

And when we did get to where Fred lived at, it wasn't no house at all. It was a store. The people had gone out of business and Fred was living in that one-room store. There was two beds in it and an old dresser and a trunk and some broke-down chairs, and that was the nice house Fred wrote us about. Water had blowed in the door of this old store, and it was just as wet in there as it was outdoors.

We couldn't all get packed up in that place. There wasn't even no place for Buddy. He had to go in a room with another boy in Sparks where the pressing-club was. Me and Fred's mother and Florrie and Jeanette stayed. Babe and Fred got a room in Sparks. They'd come every Saturday night and stay through Sunday or early Monday morning.

Poppa always had said Fred wasn't the right kind of man, and after we got to Adel it sure popped out. Come to find out right away that he didn't have the same name as his mother. Her name was Nolan. He had done some kind of devilment some time back there, and had changed his name. Even Fred wasn't his real name.

Where the big fuss come was I got so disgusted I said I sure was sorry we'd come. We'd come from such a nice house, and this place was dirty and wet and just bum. So then Babe jumped Fred about the place. The house he intended to get, he said, something had happened and he didn't. The real trouble was he'd been down there woosterpussing and harassing around, and putting all our money on his back, and trying to be in business and not knowing how. Babe asked him a thousand times what he did with the money, which he didn't appear to have any left nor nothing to show for it neither. He got right nasty about it finally, and told Babe never to ask him that any more. And she didn't.

She just started backtracking around and changing her tune to us. She told us: "Money don't mean it all to you in the world. Fred ain't the only somebody to throw away money. And he didn't aim to throw it away; he just made a mistake. And thank God there's still some for you to get when you're grown. When that time comes, if I be living, I'll see Fred won't get his hands on it."

Like Poppa had said, Fred just wasn't much of a man. He had did very well long as Poppa was there to decide things and go by, but soon as he went to doing things on his own hook he just came from together. Looked like he didn't want to work, but just to set around and depend on Babe to do. If he couldn't get the kind of work he wanted, he wouldn't work. He had just certain things he'd do. He liked to work in a tailor shop, and he'd liked it very well at the dress factory in Atlanta. But he couldn't get jobs like that in Sparks or Adel, so plenty of times he wouldn't be working a lick.

And he'd tell a story quicker than a cat can turn around. He'd say he had a big deal up, he was going to make plenty of money, and everybody would keep upset looking for it to happen—and, every time, we'd come to find out he didn't have any deal up at all. Just wasn't nothing to him.

Babe sure loved him though. The old no-account sporty-type thing. He'd bring Babe big boxes of chocolates and all such as that, but he wouldn't make a living for her.

He thought he was a big shot, running a pressing-club. Plenty of times he wouldn't take in enough at that club to buy a sack of flour; still he thought it made him a big shot and he wouldn't quit. Babe was a swift worker though, and she knew we all had to eat, and she'd wash and iron and get cooking jobs. This way we pinched through, because we didn't have to pay no rent—Mrs. Nolan owned the lot and the store. It always made me mad about Babe and Fred. Babe was the sweetest one in the family, and she got the sorriest man that ever wore out shoe leather.

One while business got pretty good at the club, but Fred was so sorry that even that didn't matter. I don't know whether he really was stomp-down no good or whether he just tried to do too many things. Once he went ahead and tried to start a woodyard. He bought a lot of wood and charcoal, but he was too lazy to chop up the wood himself, and he hired a man to saw it. Then instead of putting it in the back end of his pressing-club, he piled it up in the yard in back of where we lived. He said he wanted the club to look nice, so he wouldn't put it there. Well, he got up one morning and every bit of his wood and charcoal was gone, and he had had lots of it, too. Babe was real upset about losing all that money he'd put in it, and she told him how we begged and begged him to put the wood in the back of the pressing-club. She told him how he never paid any attention to anybody, just got mad. He got mad all over again when she told him that.

Things like that went on and it got to where it worried Babe so she got down sick. But before that happened, Mrs. Nolan heard from her husband in Salumco. Salumco is a saw-mill town; it ain't nowhere from Adel. Mr. Nolan had started a farm down there, and he used to come to Adel on Saturday nights. Mrs. Nolan got tired of staying there with just us children though, with Fred in Sparks and Mr. Nolan in Salumco, so she decided to go where her husband was. She took me and Florrie and Jeanette with her. And then a real mess come on.

Talk about falling from sugar to salt, we had sure fell in it. I never lived in a log house before in my life. It was big, but it was a sure enough log house, and cracks was between the logs and snakes and lizards would crawl in them. Lord have mercy, I purely despised that house. I despised more than the house, too.

I'd have to get up in the morning about four or four-thirty, make a fire in the stove, and cook breakfast. Old Mrs. Nolan would be lying up in bed, and I hated her guts. I'd have to cook breakfast for everybody. Breakfast was a big meal, too—fried meat, homemade grits, and I never did see no light bread there; I'd have to cook biscuits and corn-bread every morning.

I'd get out in the field about six-thirty or seven, and I'd come in about eleven and put on some bread. I'd have

picked collard or turnip greens in the garden the day before and had them cooking during the night. We'd have
this bread and greens for dinner, then back I'd go to the
field.

When we had cows, Mr. Nolan mostly did the milking.
I was scared of the cows and never did milk, but I did the
churning and straining. Mrs. Nolan never did nothing.
Whenever it rained too hard to work in the field, that was
wash day.

Some while after we went to this old hole, Babe was
taken real sick, and I went to Sparks to wait on her. She
was sick as she could be when I got there, and the way
Fred was behaving was a scandal. Sick as she was, he
wasn't a bit more coming home at night than nothing. He
had him another girl, and he wasn't studying about poor
sick Babe. He'd give us a little money for food and a doctor, but then he was through. Sometimes I'd throw him up
to Babe, but she'd tell me to stop talking about it. I know
she saw his badness, couldn't nobody help seeing it, but she
didn't want to own it.

Babe was poisoned to death, I know. One of Fred's girls
put something in her food, just like Babe seen it in a dream.
This woman had brought her something to eat—turnip
greens, potatoes, and cornbread. After the day Babe ate
that she never was no good. Then she seen the woman in
the dream putting something in the food, and that was the
very woman Fred was slipping with at the time.

She had put a spell on Babe. The doctor said he couldn't

do her no good, it was the funniest kind of sickness he ever saw. Babe was so thin; she just wasted away to nothing, and all that beautiful long black hair fell out. Her hands got just as scaly, like some kind of an animal. And she'd see things—think she saw snakes running and things like that. Sometimes we'd have to hold her on the bed, her misery would be so bad she couldn't be still.

The day she died, I went to get Fred. I told him to come right quick, that I reckoned Babe was dying for sure. This same woman Babe saw in the dream was sitting up there at the pressing-club with him, and he said he was sorry but he didn't have time to come. I knew wasn't no use fooling with him, so I lit on out and went back to Babe. She died about five in the afternoon.

We buried her the next day, and my heart was heavy as a sad cake, because looked like to me it was the nearest to nothing of a funeral somebody could have. Florrie and Jeanette and Mrs. Nolan wasn't even there; the train didn't come until after we'd done buried Babe. Fred wouldn't do a thing. He did have the grave dug, and he did borrow a mule and wagon to take Babe to the cemetery; but he didn't get no buggy or do anything to get us there and he didn't even get a preacher. Looked like he thought it was good enough for Babe to be stuck in the dirt like a potato. Some said he was worried to that, but the biggest portion of people thought he was just sorry and no good.

Wasn't nothing we could do about it though, so we put Babe on the wagon and Fred and Buddy and me walked

behind it. I reckon we'd walked half a mile right down
the dirt road when a man saw us and cut around and came
back and told us to use his buggy. That helped my feelings
some, but then a rain come up and we had to stop in front
of some white people's house on the highway. They saw
what we was at, and they called us to come in. When we
run in out of the rain, they said: "Bring the corpse in too.
Don't leave it out in the rain."

When the man found out we didn't have a minister, he
said he couldn't stand to see nobody buried the way we
was going at it. After the rain stopped he made Fred help
him put some chairs on the porch, and he preached a
funeral for Babe himself right on his own front porch. He
wasn't no God-called preacher like I wish Babe could have
had, he wasn't any preacher at all, but he gave Babe some
kind of a funeral service. Anybody'd think Fred would
have hung his head in shame, to have a strange white man
doing more for Babe's funeral than he did, but Fred just
didn't have any shame in him.

When we got to the cemetery, the grave was full of
water. We tried, but we couldn't dip much out, and we just
put the coffin down in there. Fred said he'd come back and
build Babe's grave up when the rainy weather stopped,
but, as the Lord would have it, he didn't do that either.
The police were waiting for him when he got back to
town.

He had met the train and brought his mother up to the
house. Then he walked down town and the law met him

there by his pressing-club. He didn't come back to get clothes or nothing. We never did know why the police was after him, and we haven't seen or heard of him from that day to this.

We caught the train and went on back to Salumco, me and the children and Mrs. Nolan. Buddy said he was coming down from Sparks to see us once a week, and for a while he did. Then all at once he disappeared. Just completely vanished. And then the trouble sure enough started.

It was nothing but work, work, work, and every day I'd be so tired. I just wearied of so much work, and I didn't have nothing, not even one pair of shoes. Every Saturday I'd be supposed to get a pair of shoes, but I never did. And it made me so mortified. When I'd see girls coming, I'd strike out across the cotton patch. I didn't want them to see me barefoot as a yard dog.

On top of all that, one day Mr. Nolan walked off and left us.

I was ready to fall down dead, or run till I couldn't, or anything. I wanted out. There was a Mrs. Smith helped me. She had a boarding-house, and I got acquainted with her when I went to washing for her. She used to pay me fifty cents a week for the washing, and on the day I'd get paid Mrs. Nolan would always give me a list of what to buy at the commissary with my fifty cents. Mrs. Smith told me I should give Mrs. Nolan a quarter and keep a quarter for myself. So I started doing that, and Mrs. Nolan sure raised sand.

One Sunday she told me to hitch the mule and wagon for her to go to church. Church was about twenty miles away, so I just took my chance. I got an old market basket and packed my little rags in it and went on up to the Smiths. Mrs. Smith didn't want to keep me there, but she give me a note to her sister in Tifton, Mrs. Lake. Mrs. Smith took me and put me on the train. There I set with my wore-out clothes and no shoes or stockings, and I sure looked like homemade sin tied up in a carpet rag.

Just when the train pulled out, I heard Florrie calling me to take her with me. Mrs. Nolan had got back from church and got suspicious that I had run away, and there she was at the train and Florrie and Jeanette with her. She was too late though; the train was done moving. I waved at Florrie out of the window so she'd know I didn't want to leave her.

When I got to Tifton I was scared and nervous, and the first time I lifted my eyes from the ground there was a policeman. He asked me if I was Willie Mae. I said yes, but I know I shook all over. He hadn't come to arrest me though, he had come to meet me. He said: "Mrs. Lake's fixing supper for her boarders and couldn't come, so she asked me to meet you." He said Mrs. Smith had got to studying about me after she put me on the train, and she wondered would I be too anxious and worried to know how to make it to Mrs. Lake's, so she phoned on ahead of me and told her sister I was coming. I got on in the buggy with him and he took me to the Lake House—that's what she called her boarding-house.

It covered the upstairs of three stores, just like Atlanta Life does now. She didn't have none of the downstairs, but she had the upstairs of a big dry-goods store and two other stores, and she had the widest big porch that went plumb across the front of the whole thing. It was the prettiest place I ever saw, and I felt real shamefaced about going in there as barefooted as I come in the world.

Mrs. Lake was a little bitty old humpbacked lady, and she was nice to me from the minute I got there. She fixed me a big plate of something-to-eat, and I was so hungry I eat so much I had the colic during the night.

After we finished up the dishes that first night, Mrs. Lake carried me down the street to look in the store windows. She said: "Tomorrow I'm going to get you some clothes." And she ever more than did. She bought me a pair of black patent-leather pumps with a bow on the side, and she bought me some tan sandals for everyday wear, and good and six pairs of white socks. She didn't buy me any dresses at all, because her daughters and boarders had a gracious plenty that were too little for them. They must have give me nearly a dozen dresses. And one of the boarders give me a pretty, short coat with big pockets; it was light blue and the collar was white.

Sometimes Mrs. Lake would have as many as eighteen or twenty people living there, and forty eating. And no hired help but me and Will. Will was the colored man what did the cooking. Of course Mrs. Lake wasn't like a heap of white folks now—she'd work too. So that made three of us to do the biggest portion of the work. Mr. Lake used to tend to the fires, have to get up every morning at four o'clock to do it. We didn't know what a gas furnace was then. We had a big coal-burner, and Mr. Lake would shake it down every night and have his kindling there ready for morning.

Will did all the cooking, and Mrs. Lake the cleaning. I'd peel potatoes, pick strawberries, pick turnip salads, wash dishes, and anything else that come to hand. Mr. Lake waited all the tables. Those boarders used to eat high, too. We used to buy good fresh beef for five and ten cents a pound. Beef was the regular meat, but Mrs. Lake usually served two meats.

I was there two or three weeks before Mrs. Nolan knew where I was. Mrs. Lake told me to write her, and I did. I explained to her she was so mean and hateful I couldn't stay with her no more. And I told her I had come up to Tifton to work and that I'd send her some money to help with the children. Mrs. Lake paid me a dollar and a half a week.

One Saturday Mrs. Nolan and the children come up there, and she tried to make me go back with her, but Mrs. Lake told her she'd have her locked up if she didn't let me alone. So down the steps she went, and the children crying all the way. I followed them, and I told them everything I could think of to get them quieted, but they was still crying when they left. I never did go back to Salumco, but I sent things and money regular for the children.

Finally Mrs. Nolan got it in mind to come on to Tifton to live, and she told me to look out for her a house. She wanted to move there with the children, and me to come live with them. I'd rather been nibbled in the belly by ducks, but on account of Florrie and Jeanette I went back to staying with her.

You could get a nice three-room house for three dollars a month then. We rented a good little two-room place, and we went to the furniture store and bought some things on time, and we got Mrs. Nolan a good cook job. We didn't last long though. She was still so mean I couldn't stand it, even for the children's sake, and I left and got a room with a woman named Selma Sharp.

One day I was home and was ironing on a charcoal bucket, and here come in Florrie and Jeanette. They had stole their clothes out of the house and run away from Mrs. Nolan. They had tied the clothes up in a sheet and run a broom handle through the bundle, and each carried one end of it. They were crying and ragged.

Soon as Mrs. Nolan missed them she knowed right where they was at. They hadn't been there no time when she fell in the door behind them. She got there so quick they was still crying and I was still standing there with the iron in my hand. First thing she busted in the door she hit out at Florrie, and I just throwed that iron at her. If I'd had a better aim, I'd be a murderer today. She had come to fight, and me and her tied up. I got the best of her though. I pulled the broom handle out of the children's bundle and I whammed her good. Selma got the police, which I was glad she did.

Here come the same policeman that met me at the train, and he had another one with him. Mrs. Nolan told them Florrie and Jeanette were her children and I was try-ing to take them. They told her if those girls were her chil-dren she ought to try to take better care of them. They said they'd seen those very same children poking around in garbage cans behind stores. Mrs. Nolan kept saying they was her grandchildren, but I told the policemen they was my mother's children, my little sisters. Wouldn't neither one of us hush our mouths, so finally the police said: "You both meet court tomorrow morning at ten o'clock, and, by God, you'll talk one at a time."

When we went down and met court the next day they let her talk first, I reckon because she was older than I was. She got up and said Florrie and Jeanette was her son's children and she didn't know where he was and he left them for her to raise them. Been the first lie she told, it would have choked her to death.

They listened at all her talk, and then I got up. After I said they was my momma's children, they called her back to the stand and told her if they caught up with her tell-ing a lie they'd fine her for it. Mrs. Lake was sitting right there and she spoke up and said: "Well, you may as well fine her now then, because she's telling a lie." She said: "They're not none of her children. I know that." That did it. I won the children, and it was six or seven dollars Mrs. Nolan had to pay for lying in court. They told me I had a right to take my sisters; and one of the men said, child as I was, I'd sure do better by them than Mrs. Nolan had. Mrs. Lake told him she knew I would too, and that she'd help me. Her word was better than a signed paper, too; she was just as good as good could be to all of us.

I went and got us a little two-room house from Dr. Kirk, and that's what we lived in. Mrs. Lake and others give me things for the house. Somebody give us a bed, and another lady give us another bed with a mattress and springs. Mrs. Lake give me a dresser and a washstand. Everybody then had a washstand; you just wasn't in it if you didn't have a washstand. This one had a pretty grayish marble top. I loved it, and Mrs. Lake give me a bowl and pitcher to go on top of it. Another lady give me a safe with glass doors to keep dishes in, and I bought some little fancy tissue paper with scallops and hung it on each one of the shelves. I went to the dime store and bought some material for curtains, five cents a yard. It was all white with white stripes in it. Mrs. Lake told me the curtains ought to be made full and with big hems, and she made them for me on her machine.

Some of Mrs. Lake's friends would come down of an evening and notice things I'd need, and then they'd get them for me. One gave me an odd square to put on the floor, a good wool rug. Another lady give me a table, and they just kept on until they had us fixed up. Some evenings when I'd get home there'd be so much piled on the porch I could hardly get in the door—clothes, food, wood, just about anything. And wasn't none of it no junk.

It was a year before I got that little No. 7 cook stove for a dollar, and until I did all us ate at the Lakes'. Got to where we had so much food Mrs. Nolan took to coming down for her meals. I didn't want her, but I didn't know what to do. Then Mrs. Lake told me don't feed that fool any more of her food, she'd rather anybody else to have it. I quit feeding Lizzie Nolan after that.

She held it in for me, too. One day she come over home while I was at the Lake House, and she beat the children awful bad. When I got home, welts was on them big as my finger. Mrs. Lake told the police, and they stopped Mrs. Nolan from coming there. I don't know what all they told her, but they sure stopped her from coming any more.

The children got along all right, little as they were, with me gone all day at work. The white people's Methodist church was kind of opposite to Dr. Kirk's house where we rented at. It sit up on a big hill, the prettiest red brick church, and they kept the lawn cut real neat. Mrs. Lake got the head man at the church to say that Florrie and Jeanette could play in the churchyard every day until I got home from work. I didn't have a bit of a yard myself—step off my porch and you'd be on the street—or they could have stayed at home. They couldn't carry no other child with them to play in the churchyard, but they played there every day and that kept them off the street while I was working. I'd leave food for them in the stove and they'd go get it at dinner-time.

The second winter I was in Tifton the biggest old freeze come. I couldn't hardly make it to the Lake House that morning, it was so slippy and bad. Mrs. Lake wasn't looking for me to get there. She told me about how many folks she had seen slip and fall. She told me not to ever try to come on that bad a day again. Will didn't make it there that day—he lived way out in Unionville.

Me and Mrs. Lake toughed it on out that day for the boarders and served them their dinner. By it being so cold, the pipes froze up in the kitchen and couldn't any water run through. We got some water though, and cleaned up the dishes, and I walked out on the porch to throw the dishwater out like we'd been doing. When I went to sling the pan, I slipped and whirled around and went down the steps. I was hitting each step at first, and then my foot caught in the banister and it whirled me around and I could hear the bone pop. I reckon I hung there five or six minutes before anybody saw me.

A man, as the Lord would have it, had come into the wagon yard to hitch up. He run right into Mr. Hewen's store and called him out, and Mr. Hewen said: "Oh, my

God, that's Willie Mae!" They snatched a mattress right out of the furniture store and laid it on the ground. When I fell, they caught part of me and part of me was on the mattress.

They picked me up and carried me on upstairs, and they got the doctor. Mrs. Lake just cried and took on. She knowed the children looked to me for care, and it worried her—she could see I was hurt bad. The doctor sent Mr. Lake out to our house, and they locked up the place and brought the children back to the Lake House. We stayed up there three or four weeks. They had splinted up my foot, and the Lakes bought me some crutches. When I was nearly well enough to go home, the doctor told me to stand up so many hours a day and lay down the rest of the time. I was crazy and stood up too much, and my foot didn't do well at all.

I walked on crutches for over a year. I couldn't work, of course; couldn't hit a lick at a snake. Every week Mrs. Lake would take up in the house from the boarders, and she'd bring me two or three dollars from them. All that time she was feeding me herself. My cousin Tom Cartwright and his wife had took Florrie and Jeanette out in the country with them and said they'd keep them on their farm until I was well again.

One while when I wasn't working, I wanted to go to church. Somehow or another one of my little friends got a way for me to ride. Before the sermon the preacher said: "Before I take the text, I have a letter to read to the congregation about some lost children." I was sitting up there big as you please and a-listening. And when he went to reading the names of the "lost children," it was me and Florrie and Jeanette. I got right up and went hobbling down to the front, and the preacher said the letter was from my sister Emma in Atlanta.

We hadn't heard from Emma since way before Babe died. She knowed we left Louisville, but not much after that. Next Saturday the Tifton preacher came driving up behind his white horse, and he had Emma with him.

At first the Cartwrights were real nice. But when Emma told that she was going to take the children, Lord, they fussed and argued all over the lot. Mattie Cartwright said: "Willie Mae gived us these children." Emma said I couldn't give away no children, because I wasn't of age, and Mattie was crazy. The preacher kept trying to tell them not to argue, to come on back to town and let the law handle it. Nobody paid him no mind.

Finally Emma went and broke a switch off a tree and chased the children into the buggy, and we carried them to my place with only the clothes on their backs. Next day Tom come around there with their clothes. He said the trouble was Mattie loved Florrie and Jeanette and had done got used to having them, and it really hurt her heart to have Emma grab them back that way. I was young and I didn't know nothing about how to go about things, but I sure never thought I was giving my sisters away.

Emma carried all of us back to Atlanta—she had a good

job at High's tearoom—and we stayed with her I know at least six or eight months, or longer than that maybe. We just couldn't get along though, because Sister was mean as she ever was. My cousin Pearl Cartwright and her sister came to see me one night, and they give me enough money to go to Newnan where Pearl's mother was. That was my Aunt Angeline, my momma's sister.

Soon after I went to Newnan, Sister taken sick and went to stay with Cousin Mary. Then I got a letter from Cousin Mary, and it said Sister had gone to the hospital and Cousin Mary wasn't able to see after the children any longer. She was fixing to put them in an orphanage. I sit right down and wrote Tom Cartwright and asked him if him and Mattie would take them back, and they did.

Once Sister got out of the hospital and come to Newnan to see me. She was so poor I didn't know her; she wasn't as big as a broomstick. And her eyes looked like two holes burnt in a blanket. Soon as she got there, she got sicker. She had been used to good houses in Atlanta, and she like to froze at Aunt Angeline's. She was so bad off she said she had to go right back to Atlanta, and the very next morning we put her on the train. We didn't know would she last to Atlanta or not, she looked so sick. I thought she might die right while we looked at her.

Three weeks later to the day, I got a telegram from the woman Sister lived with on Butler Street, saying to come and come at once. I run to the house where I was working at and told them, and they give me my money and over.

I bought my ticket to Atlanta—seventy-eight cents, round trip—and left on the next train, but when I got to Cousin Mary's, Emma had died.

After the funeral me and Obadiah Bunch got into it. He was Emma's beau. Emma had good jewelry, and he had stole the whole push. She had on them rings in Newnan, and she knew she was going to die and she had told me the things she wanted me to have. I was supposed to have her gold watch, her wedding set from her first husband —Doug had given her a diamond engagement ring—her bloodstone ring, and a bracelet.

Obadiah had snatched up his things and moved from the place he lived at before I could get to Atlanta. He knowed he was dirty and had stole Emma's jewelry, and he wasn't studying being where I could find him. I did, though. I was so mad I'd have walked the town over to find him. But it didn't do me no good. He must have pawned her jewelry or give it to some women, and he didn't have it time I caught up with him. I got Sister's trunk with all her clothes, and that was all. Emma's clothes were beautiful. But then they told me that by her having TB nobody could use her clothes; so I didn't get anything after all.

Soon after Sister died, I got to wanting to come to Atlanta. I'd been dissatisfied in Newnan a long time anyhow. Jobs wasn't nothing. You couldn't hardly find a job and, if you did, you didn't make nothing. One woman I worked for, I'd work all week and then she'd say: "Here's a nice dress I'd like to sell for fifty cents." It'd be so big

I could have flung a fit inside it and never popped a seam, but I'd be scared to say anything, so I'd get that big old wore-out dress and fifty cents for that week's work. Regular, every week, she'd palm off things on me that way.

The week she sold me the Rhode Island rooster I didn't get but a quarter in money. It was terrible. I was scared to say no to her and scared to go home to Aunt Angeline if I didn't. I tucked that rooster under my arm, and he sure was a buster. I got as far as the bridge before he got away from me. So when I got home, I just had that quarter and not even the rooster. Aunt Angeline tore up the patch.

I went to washing, because it was all the work I could find. I got so tired hearing them women. Time I laid eyes on them, I'd know what was coming. "Mr. So-and-So didn't get his money this week, so I can't pay you." Then they'd take the big old bundle of clean clothes and give me another big bundle of dirty ones and say: "Wash this week's clothes and then I'll owe you for the two weeks." Even when they paid, I wouldn't never get more than seventy-five cents for a great big wash.

So I said to myself: "I'm going to Atlanta if I have to foot it." I just knew I could get a better job there. I knew some white people lived on Broad Street in Newnan, and one day I went on up there and told her I was sick and needed medicine and would she please loan me a dollar. She did, and that's what I went to Atlanta on.

6

First job I had in Atlanta was for a foreign
lady. I couldn't rightly say her name then and I can't now.
Her and her husband had a store and they lived up over it.
She was dirty, but she was good. She wasn't dirty in her
ways at all, but the way she kept the house was a caution.
She'd spit all on the floor and such as that. I just didn't like
that a bit, but everything else about her I loved.

It was my job to carry out the little boy every afternoon. He was three years old, nothing but a baby really.
And the other part of my job was where I'd really have
fun: I'd help in the store.

In the afternoon when I'd come in from taking the little
boy out—he'd be tired, either I'd make him say he was
tired—I'd help in the store. People would come in for
things I could get them, like potatoes or meal, and I thought
that was the biggest thing, working in the store.

Those folks couldn't have fed me more if they'd been
fatting me up for sausage. There was candy, loose crackers, grapes, cheese—and they told me to eat as much as I

wanted. I stayed right around the cheese and nearly 'bout lived on it. It was just plain rat cheese, but much better than cheese is now.

She'd make me up a bag every evening—two or three apples, a handful of candy, some crackers, a couple of oranges. Sometimes she'd reach up on the shelf and get me a can of sardines; that would be my supper, with the crackers. And sometimes she'd put the baby back in his buggy and walk to the car stop with me.

I liked all this, but I wasn't making but a dollar and a half a week. Time I paid my carfare, I just didn't have nothing. So every Saturday me and Cousin Mary would be looking in the papers to see could we find something that paid better for me.

Hattie Bridges next door kept on deviling me about getting a job with some richer folks. She said: "Good is good, but it don't put food in your mouth or clothes on your back. For myself, I don't work for anybody but aristocrats." So she carried me to work with her one day, because her folks wanted a nursemaid for the two little girls. I told the store people a story, because I had sort of promised her I'd stay with her and besides I didn't want to hurt her feelings about the low pay. I told her Cousin Mary was sick and I had to stay home.

Hattie's folks was particular as they could be, the little old girls was bad, Hattie turned mean and hateful, and I couldn't do nothing to please nobody. I was getting three dollars a week, but I told Hattie I'd rather go back to the store and work for a dollar and a half a week. Hattie was real outdone with me and said: "You'll never amount to a hill of beans, keeping on working for poor people."

I couldn't see it her way though, so I went on back to the store people and told them Cousin Mary had done got well. She was sweet as cream to me, which I believe she really was glad to see me, and she said right away they'd pay me more money. That made me glad, because Cousin Mary had told me to ask for more and I didn't want to. Cousin Mary said, "If you ask for things, sometimes you get them." But I had heard Momma say if you asked for things, a heap of times it made it harder for you, and I believed more like Momma.

When Saturday come, they give me two dollars and a half, and I was so glad and rejoicing. Hattie was just getting three and a half for her cook job—her and her aristocrats —although she didn't work the whole day like I did. So I toed right over to her house and told her. Made her sick, too.

I got a cook job myself the next place I worked at. It was an ad job, and when I got there the lady asked me did I know anything about cooking. I told her yes'm, but I didn't. If you had a job nursing or something like that, the cooks never would give you nothing to eat fit to mention; so I had done decided I'd tell stories and get me a cook job.

She hired me, and I went to messing up the food. I called myself cooking, but I didn't a bit more know how to cook

than I knew how to jump over Stone Mountain. I was trying to learn, but I really was ruining food. Every meat
loaf or lemon pie or anything I'd mess up, I'd say: "Well,
that's the way Mrs. So-and-So made it." Finally this lady
said: "Well, Mrs. So-and-So didn't know how to cook. Do
you want me to teach you the way I cook?"

She let me watch her make a chicken pie, and then she
showed me how she wanted snap beans fixed, and we just
went on from there. Before long it come so easy to me that
I just got along fine. I liked her very well, and she ever
more than taught me how to be a good cook, but she let
me go when my vacation-time come. She wanted me to go
to the mountains with them, and I didn't want to go. She
said if I didn't go she wouldn't keep me. So I went on back
to Cousin Mary out of a job. I stayed there and rested up
some. I wasn't in no hurry. My foot would still swell up
sometimes, and I limped all the time.

That little lay-out helped me, and later I put an ad in
the paper and a Mrs. Thompson answered it. When I was
on the way out to Cherokee Avenue to see her, I said:
"Well, anyhow I know how to cook." I wasn't so worried
this time, because I did know something about it.

Mrs. Thompson said she wanted somebody to cook and
see after her little boy. There was too big boys too, but
they wasn't none of her boys, they was her husband's. She
talked so nice that I hired out to her right quick. She was

a great big woman, big-busted and heavy. I bet she weighed nearly 'bout two hundred pounds, still and yet she was pretty as a red bird. Her face was so smooth, and she had a fine suit of shiny dark-brown hair.

Mr. Thompson was a little bitty fat iron-gray-hair man, but he was nice-looking enough. They were both good to me. I lived in the house until they built me a room in the backyard. They had a heap of good scrap lumber, and they built me a nice big room out of it. I'd have to come up to the back porch to wash up, but when I took a bath I'd bathe in my room in a big tin tub. I had a little washstand, and I bought me a dipper and would carry buckets of water down. The room had two windows, and they put me a rug and a single bed in there, and a two-eyed Franklin heater. Make a fire in that heater, and it'd be so warm you could sit up with no clothes on, if you had a mind to, in freezing weather. They really fixed it up nice. And after one time when some men tried to break in there on me, they put me in a phone.

For a right smart while I was crazy about that job, but then they went to boozing and fighting. They'd fight about anything, big or little, and turned out there was plenty to fight about.

He wasn't really a Southerner like she was, and he'd go in grocery stores and buy all these little bitty spring onions and radishes and watercress and pepper grass and all such as that. Then he'd come in the kitchen, when dinner was right ready to go on the table, dragging a big bag of his weeds. One night he did that and she snatched his sack and slung it under the stove. She said "God damn it!" when she did it too, and that got it going. I went out on the porch and the little boy, Bradford, tried to get to me, but pots and pans was zooming around the kitchen so he couldn't get out.

We didn't have no dinner that night. They throwed the beef hash I'd made all over the room, and the rice and everything. They fought two hours, and when they got through they had throwed all the food away. One of the bigger boys did get a potato off the floor and eat it, but that was all anybody had that night.

I finally had to give up the job because I was scared. They both drank so much, and turned out she was crooked as a barrelful of bait worms. It sure was dirty, the way she did with those men she went with, and I knew there'd be sure-enough trouble. I should have quit before I did.

She went with two men while I was there. One was a doctor, and I don't know what the other one was. She'd tell me to hurry and clean up her room first, before the rest of the house, because she was going to have company. She didn't used to tell me that at first. At first she thought because I was young I wouldn't know what she was doing, so she'd tell me she was sick and had to stay in bed and the doctor was coming.

She had beautiful gowns, and I'd always have to put fresh linen on the bed and she'd tie a bow of ribbon in her head and put perfume on the pillows. Then she'd tell me to take Bradford to Grant Park when the doctor come.

The doctor was a great big rich-looking man in a big car. He'd have his grip in his hand and he'd say: "I'm Dr. Hendrik," and I'd tell him to go right in. She was right about me in the beginning, for at first I thought she really was sick. She'd told me she had some kind of ailment. But then I seen and learned better.

I saw how he'd go on in her room and they'd be laughing and talking, and she'd have whisky and glasses on a tray in there. Soon he'd come out and shut the front door and lock it, with me and Bradford sitting right there on the porch. I thought it would have been all right for him to shut the bedroom door if he had to give her some kind of local treatment, but then I got to studying: I certainly never seen a doctor lock the front door before.

Bradford and I would go on to the park, like she said. Bradford was three, and the cutest thing. He'd cuss worse than a sailor. Mr. Thompson used to cuss every word he'd say, and him and her would fight like cats and dogs, so, quite naturally, before Bradford could talk plain he could cuss fit to turn the air blue. It wasn't none of his fault though, and he was cute as could be. We'd stay in Grant Park a long time on the days the doctor was there. We liked it in the park and wasn't no need to come home anyhow, just to be locked out on the porch.

I had more to do with Bradford than the other two. Like I said, Buddy and Howard wasn't none of hers, they was his sons. Buddy was about seven or eight, and Howard was fourteen. Mrs. Thompson never would whip Howard, but she'd about beat little Buddy to death. Buddy did have nasty habits, but it was because they hadn't trained him. He'd have terrible colds and blow his nose on the corner of the sheets. Plenty of times she'd be in such a hurry because the doctor was coming that she'd make up his bed to help me get done and out of the house, and one day she jugged her hand right where he'd done blowed his nose.

She beat him that day till I thought we'd both die. I got beat my own self, because he'd run to me and they'd be wrassling around me, him trying to get away and her striking out. I cried harder than he did, and I'd holler: "Wait! You hitting me!" But she didn't quit. She gave us both a bad time that day.

One night after the children had all done gone to bed, she told me the details of everything about what she was doing and how Mr. Thompson was. She said he was crazy, and anyhow no one man was enough for her. I never did believe Mr. Thompson was crazy; he just drank a lot. She said she wasn't going to put up with just one man, she'd always have one or two on the side. That way, she'd never be without at least one—on the side; that way, when she quit one she'd have another. Above and beyond all that, she said, she loved good-looking clothes, and one man couldn't buy her enough.

Then she went to telling me about the doctor, and said she'd been going with him a good while. She didn't say much about the other man, just said that when either one of them was there I was to take Bradford and go to the park. That was when Mr. Thompson would be traveling on his job. When he was in town, I wasn't supposed to go out. I was supposed to sit on the porch with Bradford and watch out for Mr. Thompson. I was supposed to sit in the willow swing by her bedroom window, and if I seen Mr. Thompson coming I was supposed to knock on the side of the house. What she was going to do with that man in her bed, I don't know, but, as the Lord would have it, Mr. Thompson never did come.

He knew all about it though. Sometimes she'd go off for two and three days at the time and stay with men downtown in hotels. Mr. Thompson knowed that, too. He'd even know what hotel she was at. One night they fussed and went on so bad she got up and packed a suitcase. Buddy and Howard come crying to me about it. They called her Dearie, and they come back out to my room crying and said: "Dearie and Daddy been fighting, and they still is." We went up to the house and when she heard me and the children talking, she called me to come help her pack.

The place looked like a hurrah's nest. Glass was all over the bedroom, and the whole house was tore up. They had fought all over everywhere. I wouldn't have come out of my room 'less the children had called me. But when I got in the bedroom to help her pack, she told me she'd leave little Bradford there and get her mother to come after him and take care of him.

Mr. Thompson had cut her on the arm when he broke the hand mirror on her, and it was just laid open. She had bath towels all wet and bloody all over the place. His shirt was all tore up and his hair was wild and frizzly-looking. When I come in he said to me: "I'll kill her before it's over with. She thinks I'll say nothing while she runs around with those damn goats." He said he was glad he'd cut her arm, and then he said he'd cut up Dr. Hendrik in a very nasty way.

That was the first time I said anything. But when he said that about the doctor, I said: "You all ought to be ashamed of yourselves. I never worked for nobody went on this nasty kind of talk. I never heard talk like this till I come here, and nobody talks like that but folks what's cheap as gulley dirt."

He looked at me kindly cross-eyed for a minute, then he said: "Well, if it wasn't for her and this damn son-of-a-bitching doctor, I wouldn't be talking that way." Then he turned on her again. "Laying up in my very own bed!" he said. "Yes, I do," she said, "and I won't be in that bed with you ever any more."

At that they went to fighting again, bleeding arm and all. Buddy was wandering around the house crying, the mirror frame and pocketbooks and shoes and everything was flying, the bed was coming down, even big Howard began to holler, and I just grabbed little Bradford and got out of that bedroom. Lord, it was awful.

Turned out she didn't leave, and I just had to help her unpack her bag the next day. She sure was a case. Sometimes she'd get drunk and get out on the lawn in her bare feet and her gown all falling off and just stand there and scream. I used to could get her in sometimes; but she was so big and she could out-tussle me, so I couldn't always. Sometimes she'd do that way when he was in town and sometimes when he wasn't. If he'd be in town, that's when they'd have those bad fights.

She did do him bad, but he was bad at women too. He was all the time lallygagging around with the girls at his office, and the time come when he really stepped in his own chewing-gum. He asked a high-class girl in his office a dirty question, and she went home and told her daddy. And directly here come a long truck with seats on both sides and white men sitting all along both seats. Some had little short blackjacks and some had pistols. It scared the liver and lights out of me.

I went to the door, and they asked was he in. I told them no, and I really thought he had gone, but he hadn't. He'd seen the truck out the window and gone in the back-yard and hid in my room. They went all through the house looking for him, with little Bradford cussing at them just like his daddy. He didn't know from nothing what was going on, but he saw they was mad and he heard them cussing so he cussed right back at them. He'd follow them around while they was looking, and he'd keep on saying: "You God damn sons-of-bitches." I couldn't hush his mouth for anything.

One of them said: "This kid's going to be a chip off the old block. We ought to take him by the heels and dash his brains out right now." And little Bradford just three years old. I couldn't say: "Don't do it," or "You ain't going to do it," because I thought for sure they'd kill both of us. They'd done said they'd come to kill Mr. Thompson.

Some way or another though, they got off talking about killing little Bradford and they went to looking for Mr. Thompson again. They just took possession of the house, and used the phone and all. But they never did go down in my room. It was far from the house and there was a garden spot between, and they didn't even see it. When they'd done looked everywhere they knew to look, one of them said to me: "Tell him we been here and we'll be back." Another one said: "No, don't say that. We're not coming back." But I figured they was. They walked on off with the blackjacks and guns in their hands, and little Bradford still cussing at them all the way.

When she come in that evening, I told her about it. She said she'd heard something about it, and she said: "The least they'll do is beat hell out of him." Then she up and said: "I wish they *would* kill him." I thought she'd get her wish, but I didn't say so.

Mr. Thompson didn't come out of my place until late that night, and that was the first time any of us knew where he'd been at. He said it was a damn dirty lie what they said about him, so Mrs. Thompson asked him then why didn't he stand up to them. He said he wasn't going to have them beating on him with no blackjacks and maybe shooting him too—which of course he really couldn't have stood up and fought all those men, even if they hadn't had guns and things.

I was scared to go way back out there to my room after all that crowd of men had acted the way they did, so I stayed at the house that night. Long about one o'clock they come back, and looked like they was going to tear the doors off their hinges. I was scared. The front door and the back door were very stout, but the side door wasn't strong and that's where they was kicking and shaking the knob the most. Mrs. Thompson got up and cussed and yelled at them through the door. She wasn't scared and she wasn't really mad at them for coming after Mr. Thompson, but they was beating and banging on her door and she just naturally lit into them. Get her stirred up and she'd fight anything over a year old or a foot high. They cussed and yelled back at her and told her she better open up.

She was telling Howard to call the police and he was trying, and Mr. Thompson was getting under the bed. He stuck his head out and said: "Don't tell them where I am, for God's sake." Finally Howard got the police, and they said they'd come straight up. Mrs. Thompson was still in the hall, walking up and down and cussing and yelling at the men that she'd blow their damn brains out. Me and Bradford and Buddy went and got in a little room off in a corner. We had done had enough, and looked like it was just good and started.

Way after a good long while, seemed like, the law come. They jumped out of the car—me and the children was peeking out the window and saw them—and then we could hear foottracks running all around the house. They knocked on the door and Mrs. Thompson had a good mind not to open it, because she wasn't sure they wasn't some of them bad men making out to be the law just to get her to open the door. She finally did open up though, and a policeman come in. He went right straight through the house and let his buddies in the back door.

They said when they'd come up they'd seen some men scouting around and then jumping the fence. Mrs. Thompson told them what was the trouble and they said: "Well, where is he at?" She said: "He's in there under the bed, the dirty yellow son-of-a-bitch."

When the bluesuits went in there he was so scared. He thought they were those other men, and he kept begging over and over for them not to kill him. Still and yet, all this time he was crawling out from under the bed. Mrs. Thompson was right there when he got out, and she went to telling the police about how them men didn't accuse him of no more than he did. She was trying her best to hurt him.

While they was all talking away, everybody at one time,

those bad men came just barging on in where the police had left the door open. They wanted to tell the police on him. The man was there what owned the daughter. They still had their blackjacks and pistols, and so mad they was plumb out of their minds, and they begged the police: "Let us have him."

The police said: "If you don't get out of here, we'll lock you every one up. We got him in our hands, and you ain't going to touch him. We'll take care of whatever he did." If those police had let them have Mr. Thompson they'd have killed him dead right then and there.

The police carried Mr. Thompson on down, and by that time all us was crying—me and her and all the children, and Mr. Thompson nearly was his own self. He looked so pitiful, anybody would have cried. He was so nervous he couldn't hardly get his shoes tied.

He got out on bond or whatever you call it, and soon he was back home. When old Maria come that week to do the washing, I said: "Maria, I'm going to leave this place." She didn't pay me much mind at first; she'd been washing for them a long time and thought she knew all about them. But when I told her there was a mob crowd there and why, she said: "Willie Mae, you're too nice and young a girl to work for people like this. The Thompsons always have plenty of something-to-eat and they pay good and they're good in lots of ways, but it ain't worth this."

Then she said: "What about going out on Ponce de Leon and working for my boy out there?" And she told me about Mr. Duke then. She had raised him from a lap baby, and she still called him her boy, and now he needed somebody to help his wife with their children. I didn't pay Maria no mind at all. All I could think about right then was leaving the Thompsons.

I hadn't been spending my money, because I'd been figuring to quit even before this big mess come up. I hadn't spent nothing but carfare for a long time. Mrs. Thompson had been saving my pay for me—it was safe, she wouldn't take a penny from me—and when I quit I had three months' pay. I was going to leave on a Thursday, and I told her the Saturday before. I just couldn't tell her to her bare face that they was too dirty to work for, so I told her I was going up the country where my little sisters was. Tom and Mattie Cartwright really had taken them to New Jersey.

That Thursday morning I fixed breakfast and washed up the dishes and left before ten o'clock. Then I went to Cousin Mary's again. That's where we'd all go when we got out of a job—provided we had a little money. Cousin Mary would sleep you free, but she wouldn't feed you the first bite.

Next place I went to work was on Lombardy Way, and before long I knew I had done swapped the devil for a witch. I had put an ad in the paper and this Mrs. Prewitt answered it. She promised to pay me six dollars a week, but I should have knowed she wouldn't pay that much.

The Prewitts lived in an apartment house, and they were poor as church mice. They didn't have no phone—they used the one across the hall—and there wasn't an electric light in the apartment. They lived out of paper sacks—couldn't never buy more at the time than they'd eat right up at one meal—they'd buy ten and fifteen cents worth of wood at the time to cook with, and I never did see but two sheets in the place. I slept on a cot in what was the dining-room except there wasn't nothing in it but a big round table. They hardly had a rag to their backs. The little girl was about three, and right after I went there I took some flour sacks and made her some little drawers.

Mrs. Prewitt was in almost as bad a shape for clothes herself. She had one dress, a beautiful heavy white rayon dress with black flowers embroidered all around the tail. It sure did look good with my coat she used to borrow and she had a black velvet tam cap.

When I went out there I had good clothes and about eight or nine dollars. I had bought me a pretty shepherd's plaid coat and a white flannel skirt and a black skirt. The coat had deep pretty cuffs, and it was a good coat. I got it on Mitchell Street at one of them credit stores. Mrs. Prewitt liked this coat, which it did look good on her, and she wore it a lot. She told me Mr. Prewitt was a barber in the Candler Building and made good money but never spent a cent on his family. He never spent a cent on me either. I stayed there six or seven weeks, but I didn't get a penny of pay out of him, and they got all my nine dollars. Soon as they found out I had that money, they kept pinching it off me a little at the time until there wasn't none left.

What it was, he was spending all his money on his girl. She lived in the same apartment house as they did. She had long wavy blond hair half way down her back, and the prettiest legs I ever saw. She was a young woman, and she had a small neat waistline and big hips and bust, and the longest eyelashes. She really looked like a wax doll.

Every afternoon when they'd be coming home from work, her and Mr. Prewitt would get off the streetcar together and walk to the apartment house. They'd both of them walk right on past the Prewitts' apartment bold as a jay bird, with Mrs. Prewitt sitting on the porch, and he'd see this girl to her door and then come on back home. I reckon they drove Mrs. Prewitt plumb out of her mind.

While I was working there, a circus come to Atlanta. Mrs. Prewitt went across the hall and phoned him and said we were going downtown and at least bring the little girl to see the parade. After the parade we was all hungry, but he said he didn't have a penny. I had three dollars left, and he borrowed it. We went home and made a big pot of oyster stew. When we had done finished eating it, she said for me not to tell the neighbors they'd been getting my money from me. Looked like that made him mad, and they went on from there.

They got to arguing about could they go to the circus that night. He said no, and then he jumped up and ran down the street. She came crying in off the porch, and she said: "He's going to take that peroxided tramp to the circus, I know." Poor soul, she was just crying down. She started to put on her shoes—she had the tiniest little feet of anybody but my sister Emma—and I saw one had a hole as big as a quarter. It was a nasty drizzly night, too. Then she got my good new coat and put it on and toed right out in the rain.

When they come in they was fighting. I woke up in such a fright. They was both yelling and carrying on, and they looked a sight. She had done tore his shirt off him; he had knocked her down in the street, and my coat was all muddy and the pocket ripped nearly off. He was saying: "I've got a good mind to kill you," and looked like that gave her an idea. She stomped her little foot and screamed: "*I'll* kill *you*, you scum."

She went back in the kitchen and got the little hatchet what we cut the kindling with for the cook stove, and when she struck him it was right across the shoulder and through that big vein in his neck. He just hit the floor. Didn't never make a sound. The doctor said later she had cut his collarbone half in two. And her a little bitty frail thing, too.

After she hit him, she didn't even go over and look at him where he laid with his blood pouring out all over. She went out on the porch and started yelling: "Come and get him." Didn't nobody know who she was talking to and I reckon she didn't neither, but in five minutes seemed like every policeman in Atlanta was there. The ambulance come for him, and the police carried her down. It was late at night and I didn't have any money left, so a neighbor took me and the little girl to her house for the night.

The next day, way up in the morning, Mrs. Prewitt come home. She called me over, and I went to getting my things. She begged me not to go right then and said: "Mr. Prewitt is dead, and Mother's coming tonight." Then she busted out crying and said: "Please just stay till Mother comes," and I said I would.

We didn't have a thing to eat, and not a neighbor brought her a bite. They didn't have a bit of sympathy for her. I had one dime. Carfare wasn't but a nickel then, and I took my dime and went to Cousin Mary's and borrowed a dollar. I bought steak and sweet potatoes and fixed me and Mrs. Prewitt and the little girl a good supper.

Her mother come in after dinner, weeping and crying, a big stout old lady. She asked me about paying for the supper, and I told her about my other money too. Mrs. Prewitt said: "That's true, Mother, and there's more. I didn't have any coat and I been wearing Willie Mae's, and I've ruined it." Her mother paid me back my money and most of my salary and bought me a brand-new coat I liked just as well as the shepherd's plaid.

I stayed there until they buried him and had her trial. She come clear. Then back I went to Cousin Mary's. She said: "I hope next time you get in with some plain ordinary good folks, because you sure been having the by-Godest jobs I ever heard of."

Things rocked along and went along, and I'd go from one job to another when I had to. Sometimes I'd get a sorry one. I'd always tough it out for a right smart spell, but finally I'd think, Lord, can't nothing be worse than this; so I'd quit and go some place else, and sometimes I'd come to find out I'd done got out of the sandspurs and fell into the poison oak. And back I'd go to Cousin Mary's.

One while when I was at Cousin Mary's out of work, my cousin Veda got a pencil and paper one day and wrote out an ad, and here's the very way she put it in the *Constitution:* "Colored girl without father or either mother wants a good home with reliable people. Willing to do anything." And signed my name, Willie Mae Cartwright. She had it run three days, and it brought so many answers we had a fight with the mail-carrier.

He was my poppa's brother, and we used to fight with him anyhow. The house sit way back in the yard from Mitchell Street and he didn't want to come way back in there, and he thought by his being our uncle he shouldn't have to. He'd get right to the gate and blow his little whistle, but he just wouldn't bring that mail any farther. All us Cartwrights is contrary, and him and us used to fuss round and round. But he never fussed so much as when Veda put that ad in the *Constitution* for me.

I got letters from Texas, California, New York, and all over, and looked like everybody in Atlanta and every-whichway wrote me. People came in cars to get me until Cousin Mary made me quit going to the door. And none of them was willing to give me more than clothes and food except one in California and one in New York: them two offered me two dollars a week.

None of that was any good to me, and my money was running out. I didn't know what to do for a while. I went across the street to the Heywards. They was the colored undertakers. She let me stay there for a spell, and fed me. Cousin Mary didn't really want to fool with you once your money ran plumb out.

Then I thought about Maria what worked for Mrs. Thompson, and what she had told me about her folks out Ponce de Leon. It was a terrible long walk over to Maria's on Irwin Street, but I hoofed it there late one evening. She give me the Dukes' address and phone number, and I spent the night with Maria.

Next day Mrs. Duke rolled up in a big black car with red wheels, a seven-passenger Mitchell with a chauffeur in front. Mrs. Duke was tall but very small built, and had dark brown hair and dark blue eyes. She talked to me and we liked each other right away. She said she didn't want Georgia any more because she drank so much bust-head liquor and had hangovers, and this made her crabbish with the children. Mrs. Duke said she thought I'd do fine and that she'd start me off at four dollars a week.

She said: "I have a nice room for you downstairs, and we'll have it fixed up so it'll be very pleasant down there." So next morning out I went on the Ponce de Leon streetcar with my little pasteboard suitcase, and Mrs. Duke was waiting on the front porch. She had me to come in the front door right while Georgia was going out the back. She took me down in the basement and showed me where I'd live. The bedroom had a cute little new bed in it and a nice dressing-table. And there was a good bathroom with a tub and everything. Just for me. I thought, Lord, if I ain't swimming in deep water now. I was in my early twenties then, and I stayed with the Dukes nine years. She stuck to her word from the day she hired me up to the day I left.

She was always awful nice to me, would sell me good clothes cheap and let me use things of hers. She had a jewelry box, a great big round thing, on her dresser, and it was full of jewelry that she didn't a bit more wear than the cook stove does. I'd pick out two or three things— rings, pins, ear bobs, or a watch or bracelet—and she'd show me how to match them up pretty. She'd tell me which ones would look good together, and she'd let me wear all that stuff when I was going out and wanting to put on the dog.

One time I was really wanting to strut, and I borrowed a lot of that stuff. I put on a powder-blue evening cape

I'd bought from her sister, Miss Julie. It was a very expensive thing, and Lord knows what Miss Julie gave for it new. I had on a gray georgette dress and gray slippers, and gray dropstitch stockings for three dollars and a half—dropstitch was all the go then—and a load of Mrs. Duke's jewelry. And out I put.

I had a date to meet somebody, and there I was standing at Five Points. The policeman there said: "You sure is dressed up." He kept staring at my hands, which they really were plumb loaded with rings. He asked me where I worked, and I told him for Mrs. H. DeLorme Duke. I just spit out her name at him, because everybody in Atlanta knew they were rich.

"I don't say this is stolen stuff," he said, "but we got so much stuff out we just want to check on this jewelry." With that he took me by the arm. He wasn't rough about it, but I never had a policeman take me by the arm before. Folks standing around was just a-laughing, but it scared me to death. When we got down to the station house, the cops phoned the Dukes and I could hear him laughing over the phone. I could hear him talking too. He said: "I told her so! I told her so!" Which he had told me I'd get myself arrested some day if I kept going around loaded down like a walking pawnshop.

So it was all right, but I was still so scared I was weak. I just barely made it back to the streetcar and went home. I didn't even think about that man I went downtown to meet until way after I had done got back home.

All that was back in the time of that other world war, and I was a little bit worried about my real boyfriend, Harry Roberts. I was going with him steady, and Mrs. Duke thought he was some punkins. She said I was hateful to him and snooty, and I guess I was some. Everybody was being drafted in the Army, but some way I didn't much think Harry would have to go. Then one night he come out there and said: "Well, I got my word today. I got to go." Oh, I hated it so bad. I didn't know how I cared for Harry until Uncle Sam got him. He went out to Camp Gordon, and I'd go out there on Thursday evenings to see him. Finally they shipped Harry overseas, and I like to died.

Harry and I would write letters though and things would have been fine if some old jealous-hearted busybody hadn't butted in. I was going with another boy, and somebody wrote Harry and told him, and I never heard from Harry again. Not one other letter. I knew he hadn't got killed, because his mother got letters from him. If I thought I like to died when he got shipped overseas, I didn't know from nothing. When he quit writing me is when I really like to died.

Seemed like I didn't have any sense any more. I never did hardly know what I was doing, and I didn't care about doing nothing anyhow. I remember one morning me and Mrs. Duke was fixing breakfast. She always helped me with breakfast. The children were crazy about grits, and we'd soak them overnight so it wouldn't take long to cook them in the morning. That morning the water was just about boiling and I went to take the box of salt and put some in. I had the box in my hand, shaking it in the grits and stirring, and I saw the grits getting foamy but seemed like it didn't make no impression on me. Mrs. Duke said: "Willie Mae, for pity's sake, do you see what you're doing?" I seen she was staring at my hand, and I looked too and saw I had a box of washing-powder in my hand and the grits was yellow as gold. We got something else for breakfast that day.

Mrs. Duke went to studying about me then, and finally she said: "Willie Mae, don't you want a vacation? Wouldn't you like to go to Newnan for a couple of weeks?" I said I guessed I would, I didn't care. She said: "Well, let's plan on that, and we'll give you a go-away party on your birthday."

She ever more than gave me a party too. It was the biggest party I ever saw in my life. Jesup and Antrum sold the best ice cream, and Mr. Duke ordered three or four gallons from them. Mrs. Duke got individual cakes, little square white cakes with a pink W on each one. The Dukes and Miss Julie were at the party the first part of the night. All my friends come and more besides. I know there was every bit of seventy-five people at the party, in my room and in the playroom and out in the backyard. We played cards in my room and the playroom. The Dukes had a victrola in the playroom and lots of records.

The bed was just loaded with presents. Mrs. Allison, Mrs. Duke's mother, gave me three yards of French ging-

ham, the first time I ever had French gingham. The Duke
children gave me five dollars apiece. Mr. and Mrs. Duke
gave me a check for sixty dollars and a month off. I sure
thought I was it that night.

I was dressed fit to kill, too. I had on a mustard-yellow
georgette dress with plaid on the bottom. Oh, it was the
prettiest dress. And tan patent-leather slippers and my
good dropstitch stockings. My hair—it was good and a
foot and a half long then—was fixed pretty as a peach. I
couldn't get up to Mrs. Harris on Baker Street to get it
fixed for the party, but Mrs. Duke could curl it better
than her anyway. Early in the evening before the party,
I set in the chair and Mrs. Duke heated up that electric
curler of hers and when she finished the curls laid so pretty.
I had a bright comb in my hair that night too. It was
nothing but Kress stuff, but it sparkled.

Where we lived at on Ponce de Leon, the streetcar
stopped right at the door. That night it just cold out un-
loaded there, and it was nothing but soldiers from Camp
Gordon. They come down the driveway like a herd of
horses with those big heavy shoes. That was the night I
met my husband.

Verlee was the cause of my meeting him. She was the
Dukes' laundry woman. I had done told her during the
week that I wanted her and her husband to come to the
party. She said her baby was sick and she'd have to stay
home, but Charlie could come and bring his brother. I had
my trunk all packed—I finally decided to go to New

Jersey where the Cartwrights had moved and taken Florrie and Jeanette with them—and I wasn't interested in meeting no man anyway. I was still sick over Harry. But Charlie came to the party, and he brought Dan Workman with him.

They both had on gray suits, white shirts, and black ties. They looked mighty good, but Dan looked the best. Oh, Dan just looked at me and I looked at him. I couldn't talk to him much though because I had a boyfriend there, Tom Cuthbert, and Tom had give me a wonderful present. I didn't care nothing about Tom, which he knew it very well, but I couldn't have ditched him right that night for Dan, and me just barely setting eyes on Dan. Everything and everybody was so wonderful that night, and then Dan came and I couldn't quit looking at him—I felt like I was going round like a windmill on a stick.

I went on up to New Jersey to see Florrie and Jeanette, and I stayed in Camden with them a couple of weeks. Then I came back to Atlanta and met my friend Minnie and we went to Jacksonville for two more weeks. The night I got back from Jacksonville, Verlee called and said Dan wanted to see me. I didn't care nothing about seeing him. I had done forgot how I got the dry grins just looking at him that night at my party, and my clothes wasn't pressed or nothing, and my vacation hadn't done me no good. I was more worried about Harry than before I left. I was so upset I was going to leave the Dukes; I didn't have any mind to work, and I didn't know what to do. And I had cut my hair off in Jacksonville, maybe because it was so hot or either because I didn't half know what I was doing.

Verlee kept on at me though, and finally I said I'd meet Dan at Ponce de Leon and Highland. I did, and we went to Cousin Mary's. We sit there and talked a while. Then Cousin Mary got me out on the back porch. She said: "Willie Mae, name of God, where did you get that old man from?" I said: "Dan ain't so old." She said: "He's good and twenty-five years older than you. He's been married and divorced. He's got two children." I don't know how did she find out all that, but I didn't ask her. I didn't like it what she said, and that just upset me all the more.

I was still calling myself working for the Dukes. Some days I'd work there all day, but I couldn't sleep in that room. That was where Harry used to come to see me, and looked like I could still see him sitting there in that willow rocking-chair. I slept at my friend Eleanor Walker's, and every night I saw Dan.

One Saturday evening we went to the Grand Theatre; colored people could go there then. I had on the prettiest suit; I'd bought it in Jacksonville. It was light-weight, soft blue wool with big white buttons, and it was a honey. It was lined inside with white silk. Dan and I were sitting up in the show and he said: "I want to ask you a question." I had gone to thinking about Harry, so when he broke in on me like this I looked at him just as hateful and didn't say a word. He said: "What about us getting married?" I said: "You ain't talking to me. There's only one man in the world I'd marry, and he ain't in the United States." Dan looked just as pitiful, and after that he didn't say any more, just looked at the show.

After the show he carried me back to Eleanor's and he said: "Ain't no need of me coming back any more." I said: "No, there ain't. Not if you're looking to get married." But the next Sunday night he was right back, and every time he changed suits he got better looking. He was tall and broad shouldered, something like the way my poppa and all his brothers was built, only he wasn't quite as heavy as them.

I got to studying about Dan. He had a good job. He had a white man's job—checking lumber at the Patillo Lumber Yard. He was a good steady man, and sweet as he could be, and he sure thought I was the only gourd on the vine. I talked to my cousin Pearl Cartwright about him, and she told me she didn't see where forty-five was all that old like Cousin Mary said. And I talked to the Dukes about him. One night we was in the kitchen sitting at the table and Mrs. Duke said: "When are you coming back to work?" I said I just didn't know—that nor nothing else.

She saw I was troubled, and she said: "Willie Mae, you just have to give Harry up. I liked Harry too; he's a nice fellow, and we don't know what's wrong now, but you just have to make yourself get him off your mind." I said I didn't think I should marry Dan, but I was study-ing about it. I had done told him this. I said I was afraid I wouldn't treat him right because I was still in love with

Harry. Mrs. Duke said again she thought I'd have to forget about Harry. "But," she said, "I'll tell you something else I think. If I were you I wouldn't marry Dan. He's too old for you." Mr. Duke had come in the kitchen while we was talking and he said: "Bertha, you don't know a thing about Dan's age." She said: "I don't care. Willie Mae oughtn't to get married just because she's dissatisfied." I didn't hardly know what to think. I felt like I'd been stirred with a stick.

Then Dan said he wanted to take me to see his momma and poppa. He told me: "My poppa heard I was going with you, and him and Momma wants to meet you." I went on with him, and his momma tried to give me everything— ham, eggs, quilts, and everything she could think of. They had just made sure we was going to be married. I didn't tell them I was either I wasn't, and they didn't ask me. The next Sunday Dan come by the house and said he'd see me that night. When he got there that night he said: "Any time one of us gets married, my poppa gives us fifty dollars and fifty dollars for the girl. I brought you yours."

That Sunday we went on to see his family—they lived on the other side of Decatur—and we had the best dinner. His father asked me if I was going to live on the lot at the Dukes' or in town. I said in town. He told me anything they could do, help us out with anything we needed, he'd be too glad to do it. And she was telling how she'd furnish cover for us and all the hog meat we wanted.

That evening I went back to Cousin Mary's and told her. She had changed up and gone to liking Dan and she was tickled to death, but my uncle started it again about Dan being too old for me. He used to be around at Cousin Mary's a lot, and he had done heard her talk that way when me and Dan first started going together. I told him I knowed how old I was and I knowed how old Dan was, and I wasn't doing nothing I didn't know about.

I couldn't half work on Monday for telling Mrs. Duke about it. She was fussing and she said I was the biggest fool. She knew I wasn't going to be working any more like I had been, and then too I believe she really didn't think me and Dan matched up very well. Little Rodney, he didn't like it either, and he just cried. He was going on four then. He said: "When he comes in the driveway to get Willie Mae, I'm going to shoot him."

My friend Eleanor Walker asked me to get married at her house. She had a nice little living-room and a piano. The next Thursday I just acted like it was my evening off and we went on to Eleanor's and got married. We laughed and said our honeymoon was at the Grand Theatre, because we went to the show that night. Eleanor and her husband and five or six of us went. I was too excited to even think about the show, but we all went. Dan and me stayed at the Walkers' that night.

*　　*　　*

Next morning I went to the Dukes'. I wanted to tell her and I didn't want to tell her. I didn't want to hear her fuss no more. She was getting ready to go to town and in the biggest kind of a hurry. I couldn't hardly hold her there long enough to tell her; I had to follow her on out in the driveway to the car. When I did tell her, she just sat there.

Then she said: "I don't know exactly what to think, but I don't appreciate this." She said I didn't recognize her rights and I ought to have told her. Which I had been telling her over and over and finally quit because she fussed so much every time. Mr. Duke didn't feel that way. That night he said to her: "Bertha, I don't understand you, the way you don't want Willie Mae to be married. You got married." She said yes but she had let her mother know ahead of time. "Well," he said, "Willie Mae hasn't got a mother, and I think it's all right the way she did."

Mrs. Duke pouted around two or three days. She wasn't real nasty, but she wasn't the same. Later she asked me if me and Dan would like to live on the lot, and I told her no; Dan didn't like to live on white people's places; Dan always said every tub ought to stand on its own bottom. We went to looking for an unfurnished bedroom, but I was still staying at the Dukes' while we looked.

Next Thursday I went to the Peoples Furniture Store on Decatur Street and paid down on some bedroom furniture. Quite naturally they asked me where I worked and such as that, and when they telephoned Mrs. Duke she sure knocked me. She told the furniture man she didn't think me and Dan would stay together, she didn't believe Dan was a worker, and all such as that. That put the man betwixt two opinions letting us have the furniture, because it was a lot of money—two hundred dollars and something, fifteen down and two-fifty a week. But he took a chance on us and let us have it. We found us a room on Little Street in Summer Hill.

I stayed working for the Dukes, and she got over her mad and went to acting like she used to. She had a big storage room just filled with good stuff she wasn't using, and she told me to get in there and take whatever I wanted. I got some vases, a solid mahogany chair, two lamps, sheets—not at all bad, just thin—and two bedspreads, brand-new, what had been given to her. And dishes. I always was a fool about odd teacups and saucers, and she give me just a big stack of them. After work that day she took it all home for me in her big car. Our room was large but it had been looking kind of skimpy, and these things filled it out and made it much better. Next week her mother gave me a big rolltop mahogany desk with a place underneath where we kept our shoes.

Dan and his divorced wife never did quit being friends. Him and Avis were so young when they were married they just didn't have sense enough to work things out, and they had done been divorced for years before I met him. I didn't want to meet her after we was married. I was very nasty about it, because I thought she'd act crazy like me; but come to find out she had more sense than me, and we got to be close friends. We met at one of their kinfolks' funerals.

We was going to the funeral and we run into Avis at the barber shop where the funeral cars were parked at. Eleanor had to go to the bathroom and there wasn't no place closer than Avis's house. They say women can't hold council because some of them always got to be going to the bathroom, and it's the dying truth. I kept trying not to go to Avis's house, but Eleanor was my bosom friend and she said she wasn't going to ruin her kidneys on account of me, and she purely made me go with her.

Looked like Avis couldn't be friendly enough. Looked like she could have poured cream on me and eat me with a spoon. She showed me a cigar box she had cut a slit in and painted right pretty, and said she and Dan had used to save money in it. I didn't enjoy that a bit, but she was so nice to me I couldn't keep from liking her. So we all went on together, and me and Avis nearly broke up the funeral.

Time we got there folks weren't studying about the corpse any more, they was looking at her and me and Dan. They went to whispering all over. Avis said: "Look at them, Willie Mae. They just gossiping about you and me, ain't they?" I didn't talk much because I was still half mad with her, but that sort of tickled me so I went on and made friends with her.

Dan went in the church between me and Avis, and the deacons and everybody else was peeping and whispering. Except one old hootnanny, she talked out loud. She said: "Bless God, here comes Dan Workman with both his wives!" And after the funeral everybody crowded around and was hugging and kissing me and Avis and talking about how nice we were to be friendly. I didn't see nothing extra about it, and all that talk got me mad again.

Along about a year later, me and Dan moved out of the room and got a three-room apartment in a house on Dunlap Street. So we had to get more furniture. The first Saturday I was off, me and Dan's daddy went to town together and we walked around looking for a stove. I didn't want no wood stove, because I didn't want to get up and have to make a fire every morning. Mr. Workman said: "I used to work at the Gas Company years ago. Let's go up there and look at some of them stoves." We looked at the ranges, and he paid five dollars down on a nice gas stove and told me if we ever couldn't make the payments he'd do it. They was five dollars a month. This stove was a Detroit Jewel; in them days they was the best stoves going.

While we was doing all this shopping, Mr. Duke said: "Willie Mae, I never did give you a damn thing, did I? You go downtown and pick you out a breakfast suit and charge it to me." My next day off I walked and I walked and I walked, and then I found me a breakfast suit, an oak table and four chairs. It was thirty-five dollars and Mrs. Duke said: "I think we can do better than that. Let me help you look." She didn't find one that day, but one day soon she said: "I found a beautiful suit and one I know you'll like." It was second-handed but you couldn't tell it from new, and for thirty dollars she had got me a table, four chairs, and a little buffet thing to keep dishes in. She tagged my name on it, and when I saw it I was so rejoicing that I hadn't got the one I found—this one was mahogany.

Our kitchen was the cutest thing. I had a nice blue-checked linoleum square in there. All the children in the neighborhood took up nickels and dimes and bought me a big garbage can. I had blue-check curtains trimmed with red rickrack, and Mrs. Duke brought me a roll of wall-paper and I fixed up my kitchen closet. I had the best-looking kitchen in the apartment house.

The other room just had little odds and ends, and we had to wait a while to get that fixed up. I did buy a little old daybed so Dan's father could come and spend Saturday nights with us. When I got to wanting to fix up my front room nice, Mrs. Duke said I shouldn't go into debt about it because she had a green bedroom suit she didn't use. It was the prettiest one you most ever saw—a bed, dresser, chifferobe, a bench for the dresser, and an odd chair. All it was was dusty, and time I washed it off with Ivory soap it looked like a million dollars. Since she had give us all the furniture, we bought a rug at the furniture store, new; it was cream and green with wreaths all on it.

Not long after we moved in the apartment, here come Tom Cartwright to Atlanta with Florrie and Jeanette. He said Mattie had come down sick in New Jersey. I didn't know Florrie no more than if she'd been somebody from New York. They'd left Jeanette at my cousin's on Mitchell Street, and when I asked how come they did that Florrie told me Jeanette was so sick she didn't know day from night. We went right on out to Mitchell Street to see her. They had done got a doctor. What it was, up there in New Jersey it was cold and she didn't have enough clothes; she was loaded with cold, and a gland on her neck was big as a hen egg. Come to find out Tom was really after getting rid of them children.

I flew to the phone and called Mrs. Duke, and she said she'd come next morning. She come on up on Dunlap and got me in her car, and we went and found Jeanette was a little bit better. Poor little old thing, she was only not quite eleven years old. Mrs. Duke got her own doctor out there and he said Jeanette should have been taken care of way before then and she'd have to go to the hospital. He couldn't get her in the Grady, he had to take her out to Battle Hill because she had a TB gland. He got the papers fixed up and took her out there, and little Jeanette said she thought she'd get better there. But a couple of days later she took deathly sick and the next night she died about eight o'clock.

The Dukes was the best folks in the world. She brought Jeanette everything to be laid out in—a slip, pants, white socks, the prettiest white dress, and a wide white satin ribbon for her hair. He called Cummings on Auburn and Piedmont and told them whatever I wanted in a reasonable amount to let me have it and send him the bill. I had two ten-cents policies on Jeanette; one paid forty dollars and one paid fifty. I got her a pretty plush dropside casket that let down and you could see her from head to foot. The bill was close to two hundred dollars. I asked Mr. Duke did he want me to pay him back by the week or by the month, and he said: "I don't want you to pay me a damn cent. I buried Jeanette myself."

We sure appreciated it, and after that Dan would go out there on Saturday evenings and cut the grass, keep the basement clean, wash the car, and all such as that, and never let them pay him a penny. We worked at things together, us and the Dukes. That winter we was trying to get some coal, and I told Mr. Duke I wanted a ton because buying it by the sack cost too much. When I got home that evening, the ton of coal was there and a whole lots of kindling. We didn't never have to buy no coal, and they didn't have to pay nobody to cut grass and all that.

We got along that way two or three years and then I had to quit the Dukes. I had done got so tired I had to stop. I did keep doing the laundry, but Mrs. Duke got another woman to do the cooking. I got to thinking I was going to have a baby. I stayed sick all the time, and soon I found out I really was that way. Mrs. Duke said she was proud for me, and I'd go out to her house and make baby clothes on her machine. I called her house my other home.

Those nights I sewed baby clothes I didn't have no supper to fix for me and Dan; Mrs. Duke would always give me a big pail of food when Dan would come by for me.

She got me a bed in the Grady and she come to the hospital the day I went. I stayed two days in the ward and they sent me home, and then I had to go back again. They said I was having trouble because I'd worked too hard after I was pregnant. The second time I was there a day and a half before the baby was born. The doctor was putting something on my face—they was putting me to sleep —and kept asking me things like where I lived and what was my husband's name. I told him I lived at the Georgian Terrace Hotel, and I said Dan's name was Zack or Hack or some such foolish thing, and I believe that's why they got Dan's name wrong down there to this day. We found that out when Viola and Joyce went to get their birth certificates.

Hal was a big fine baby, and I just had to go show him to everybody, and I know I killed him taking him all around that cold December. He didn't live two months. One doctor said he had spasms and convulsions, but another one said it was plain old pneumonia. I didn't know how to take care of a baby then, and I'd let everybody in the neighborhood hold him and play with him, and I know we killed him from not knowing any better, and it nearly run me crazy.

Mrs. Duke made all the funeral arrangements. I was so broke up over letting Hal die that way, I just sit there and didn't do a thing. She buried him, just like Mr. Duke did Jeanette, and I never even knowed how much it cost.

Florrie had been living with me and Dan ever since Tom brought her and Jeanette down from New Jersey. She was going on fourteen then and I tried to make her go to school, but she wanted to work. She said she hated to be sitting down on Dan, big as she was. She had boys in her head more than books too, and she wanted to work so she could have nice clothes. Pretty soon she went to courting. I went back to working at the Dukes.

Wasn't a year after Hal died that Viola was born, in February. I was washing curtains soon one morning when that pain hit me. A neighbor called the Grady ambulance for me. Thirty-eight women was in that ward, and they were just having babies right and left. They were bringing them in and taking them out all day. That noon they moved me out and I lay tied down on that hard table—that's how they used to do—so hungry I didn't know what to do. Viola was dry labor and they kept thinking she was coming any minute, but nothing happened.

It got to be eleven that night, and I hadn't had a thing to eat all day. I told Dr. Gordon, and he said that didn't make sense. He went down the hall, and then here come a colored orderly with a trayful of eggs, bacon, toast, and milk, and I ate like a field hand. Then I went to sleep for a few minutes.

That doctor sure was nice, and he stayed with me and talked to me a lot while we was waiting. Once he said:

"It's quarter to twelve now, and you at least wait fifteen minutes more because today's the 13th. You wait fifteen more minutes and you'll have a valentine." I went on back to sleep and this time I slept until early morning. About five-thirty them pains went to rapping on me so I thought I was seeing judgment day. Everybody come with caps on their heads and things around their mouths. Wasn't nothing around my mouth though, and I sure hollered that hospital down.

Viola was black as any ink poured out of a bottle, and had hair nearly down to her shoulders. She had the heaviest head of hair you ever saw on a baby, and it was pretty and straight, too. I was more particular with Viola than with little Hal, and she got along just fine.

I quit the Dukes after she was born. Dan had left his truck-driving job with the Morris Transfer moving-people, and gone back to the Cable Piano Company.

In a couple of years I got pregnant again, and I was tickled to death. I went to the hospital to take treatments, because they said to do that and I'd get along better. All the same I had a worser time with Joyce than Viola, all because I wanted a nice clean house. The walls was awful dirty and the landlady wouldn't clean them, so I calcimined all three rooms myself a couple of months before Joyce was born. I didn't make it to get the bathroom fixed. It was painting overhead on the ceilings that was so hard on me, I think. After that I wasn't no good, just dragged around to the hospital and back.

The doctor asked me what had I been doing to be in that shape, and he sure flew up when I told him. "Clean walls!" he said. "Well, you may have worked yourself right on to a clean cooling-board."

About seven o'clock one evening I called my neighbor and asked her to call the ambulance. I hadn't looked for the baby that day, but I was hurting so bad that evening that I knew I had to go. When the doctor that come on the ambulance saw me, he said: "My Lord, we got to be quick." One of Joyce's feet had done pushed out and there she was coming feet foremost, and I was hurting so bad I was blind as a bat. They put me in the ambulance and off to the hospital we flew. While we was on the way, all of a sudden things turned dark and I didn't know nothing else till after Joyce was born. They must have put me to sleep at the hospital, because I didn't know nothing about having the baby.

It must have been around nine the next morning when I begin to come to myself. A doctor was sitting by the side of the bed and he said: "You're going to be all right, and the baby's all right, but you sure did have one hell of a time." Besides Joyce coming feet first, her navel cord was wrapped around her neck. They had had to take her, and I had thirteen or fourteen stitches. After that I didn't particularly want no more babies.

The landlady felt so mean about the walls she hadn't cleaned that she said she knew had caused all that trouble that she gave us a month's rent free. I began to get on

pretty good and things were working all right. After I
got stronger, Dan—he was always so kind and nice—Dan
sent us to see this friend of mine in Jacksonville. Joyce
was nearly six months old then, a good-sized arm baby.
I taken both her and Viola, and we stayed nearly three
months down there. Dan couldn't go at all, but he was
glad to send us.

When we come back home, looked like everybody was
moving out of the house and getting better places to live.
I just couldn't get acquainted with the new ones, so Dan
said: "Well, get out and find us a place you like." My
friend had come home with me from Jacksonville, and me
and her with the children in the pushcart walked around
until we found a house on King Street. It was a house
with four apartments in it; each apartment had four rooms
and hall and bath, the nicest place we ever lived in.

Soon after we moved in there I got pregnant again, Lord
have mercy. When Julius was born he lived in an in-
cubator a day and a night, and the next morning the nurse
found him dead. Julius was a good-sized baby, as big as a
good big rabbit, but he was born ahead of time and he just
wasn't strong enough to tough it out.

Our rent was so high—$32.50 a month—that I taken in
a couple of roomers to help out on it. Then I went to
stretching curtains for folks and doing a little sewing. I
wasn't much of a hand at sewing, but I could do some

things. We were getting along all right till all at once one day Dan come home from work and said: "I haven't worked today worth a thing. I been laying down nearly all day." They was moving a piano, and one of the men's hands slipped and the piano mashed Dan some way. He thought he had strained his shoulder too. There wasn't no mark at all on him, but his chest hurt him awful bad. He went to the Cable Company's doctor, but seemed like he didn't get better. After that sometimes he couldn't go to work but one day in a week, and then again sometimes he'd go three or four weeks and work straight on through. When he got plumb down, we moved out of that apartment because we couldn't keep up the rent with Dan laid off from work.

We moved to Dunlap Street again, but in a different house. It was an upstairs apartment, fourteen dollars a month. Dan was down for two months and more. We was getting some insurance money, and the Cable Piano Company gave him his pay for most of that time too. When it dragged on so long, they went to giving him half pay— because he had been with them a long time and he had got hurt at work.

I'd have to sit up so much at night with him. Seemed like things never did go right. Sometimes there'd be too many people there, and sometimes nobody at all would be there to sit up with him some so I could get some rest. Florrie begged me to bring Dan and the children and come live with her. She had married John D. Peters right after

Julius died, and they had a nice place on Newman Street. They was downstairs, and had a big yard where the children could play. I put all our stuff in storage except one bed and the daybed, and we moved down there with her and John D.

Dan could get up some and drag around, and he'd set out on the porch some. Later he went back to work, and worked off and on for nearly three months. Viola was seven then, and had just entered in school; and days when he couldn't make it to work, he'd try to take her to school. Some days he wouldn't get plumb there with her, and he'd have to stop and sit on different people's porches before he could get back home. So I stopped him from going with Viola, and after that he'd stay on the porch and see after Joyce—she was five then. Dan never was any hand just to lay out and do nothing at all.

Truth to tell, he used to work when he should have been down flat of his back. He worked the day before he died. Seemed like he just wanted to go that day, so he did. They didn't let him do no lifting, just drive the truck. Even Dan couldn't tough it out that day though. When he come home he said, and he was real down in the mouth about it: "If I don't never get well and we just end up outdoors, I'm not going back to work as sick as this. I was hurting so bad today I run right through a red light."

I had some uniforms to make for some girl with a maid job, and I pulled the machine out after I had done put the children to bed that night. Dan said: "Just for tonight,

I sure wish you wouldn't sew." I said: "If you don't want to hear the machine, I won't." And I closed it right back up.

Then he said: "Write Emma a letter for me." This was his sister in Oklahoma. I got the paper and pencil and wrote the letter, but I couldn't get it off that night because I didn't have no envelope. Dan told Emma in the letter that he didn't get no better and he sure wished he could see her, and he thanked her for the money. Every so often she'd send us two or three dollars, sometimes five.

All the time Dan had been sick, I'd hardly ever take my clothes off at night. That was because I'd have to get up with him a lot, and those houses we lived in were cold. But, of all those nights, that one night I pulled off my clothes to go to bed. All us went to sleep. Florrie and John D. had been gone to bed since about ten o'clock; they slept in the front room. The children was in the double bed where I slept with them; Dan was on the daybed by the window. Well, I pulled off my clothes and covered up the fire in the grate so it wouldn't burn out so fast. Looked like to me I hadn't been laying down five minutes when Dan called me to get up quick. We had a light hanging down from the ceiling, and I couldn't find the cord to save my soul. Before I could get it or either find a match, Dan had done hit the floor, wham.

I struck a match to find the light cord, and when I got the light on he was laying right down flat on his face. I run and called Florrie and John D. Dan was big, and even John D. couldn't get him up off the floor, so he called

Tommy Row from next door and they laid him on the bed. Time they got him on the bed though, Dan was dead.

I won't live where somebody died, and the upstairs apartment was vacant, so I moved up there. Florrie and John D. moved with me, and we lived up there a year or two. I was wanting to go to work, but the children was still so small that I couldn't work in no peace with somebody else keeping them. I thought about all the things Dan had said about the Masons and I thought: "Well, now is the time I need them people's help." I called the master of Dan's lodge and told him I wanted him to come out and explain to me about the Masonic home for children. Ordinary folks couldn't send their children there, just the Masons. He said it was the best thing, for them to go to the home. He told me they'd be sent to school and everything, and it sounded real good. So I went to work and got them ready and carried them down to Americus.

We went to a great big building and there was lots of little girls. Viola liked it right away. All three of the buildings looked nice outside, but two wasn't nothing on the inside. I left Viola and Joyce there thinking they'd be in the good one, like the woman promised me. Viola was so excited about all the girls she could hardly take time to tell me good-by, but Joyce was crying and didn't want me to leave her.

Back in Atlanta, I wanted a job to stay on the place after

Viola and Joyce was gone, and I got me a job with a Mrs. Warner with a room on the lot. It was a nice little room in the attic. She'd give me books to read and all, and she was very nice. I was upset about Viola and Joyce though; seemed like them and Dan had done left me all at one time. One night about a month after I'd taken them to Americus, while I was asleep both those children come to me just as straight, and both of them had a little red candle lighted in her hand. It was their spirits, I reckon. Next morning I said: "Mrs. Warner, I got to go to Americus. They're either sick or something's wrong." She told me it was just a dream and tried to talk me out of it, but she couldn't. I was going to see about my children and couldn't nobody hinder me.

John D. had a little truck, so he and Florrie and I got on the road soon that morning. When we rolled up at the Masonic home, I didn't see my children playing out. The teacher said she'd get them cleaned up and bring them to me. I said: "Don't wait for no cleaning up. I want to see them." When she brought them in I was so disgusted. Viola came kind of sliding in the room and just said: "Hey, Momma," that was all, and she looked like she was cowed down. Their dresses was all but tore up and hanging in strings, and they was both nasty dirty. I know all children going to get dirty, but these children had done *been* dirty for a long spell, and mine had never been in that kind of a shape before. They was just hard-down dirty, and dirt was even caked in their hair. Joyce fell up in my lap and

commenced to hollering to be taken home, and she was so
excited and upset that soon she nearly puked her guts out.

After that happened, the teacher sent for some older
girls to give them baths. Then we went to the dining-room
to eat. They had chicken and dressing and Irish potatoes
—they raised everything they cooked there—and some
kind of pudding for dessert. I thought I smelt something
tainty, but I couldn't tell just what. Joyce come in and sit
beside me and asked me if I brought that chicken. I said:
"Haven't you already had any?" She said: "No, We've ate,
but we didn't have no chicken, just some kind of old stinking meat." Then I knew I was right. My mind had led me
to go down there.

I got through my dinner and went out in the sitting-
room with Mrs. Hubbard, and she said they always liked
for the parents to let them know when they were coming.
"That gives us a chance to have the children nice and tidy,"
she said. I thought: "It would have took you a week to
get mine nice and tidy, the mess they's in, but they ain't
going to be here much longer."

Mrs. Hubbard said we could spend the night there, and
she made us acquainted with Mrs. Booker. She was a big
fat black woman, sweet as she could be, and when I met
Mrs. Booker I met a friend. She and her husband taught the
big children there. I said: "Mrs. Booker, this isn't a good
place, is it?" And she said: "*No.*" She said if I'd spend the
night with her instead of in the guest room she'd tell me
everything about it. I found out why Viola and Joyce

wasn't in the good building but in a very bum one. They had rooms in that good building all right, but Mrs. Hubbard was holding them back for when some rich Mason died and left children; nobody poor like mine would get them.

Me and Mrs. Booker talked all night long. She told me the children didn't get a bath but once a week, and she said the biggest portion of the clothes they had brought with them had been taken and distributed out to other children. They were sleeping in the bed with a third girl, and a hole in the floor under the heater where they slept at was big enough to put a hat through. Sometimes Viola would ask for more bread, but she never got it. Mrs. Booker said: "Folks got to send more than a dollar a week for Mrs. Hubbard to take any care of their children."

I had been told I wasn't supposed to have to send any money at all, but I had sent what I could—a dollar each week. Mrs. Booker said there was this girl would get my letters out of the mail, even though they were backed to Mrs. Hubbard or to her, and she'd take the dollar every time she could.

Mrs. Booker said for me to go back to Atlanta and see Dr. Walters. She said she was up there once and slipped in his office and seen where he hadn't signed all the papers, and Viola and Joyce didn't really have no business at the home. So she said I shouldn't have any trouble getting them out. We come on home then, and Florrie and I talked it over.

This friend of mine on King Street, Maggie Green, the one that claims to know so much, said she was sure Dr. Walters didn't know things was that way down in Americus. So me and her goes up to his house to see him one night. He had been a surgeon, but then he was old and retired. He was such a big shot you had to make an appointment to see him. He went to pawing in his files, but he couldn't find no record on Viola and Joyce. He was awful mad at what I told him about conditions, and he really tore up the patch. He said to Maggie: "Mrs. Green, this woman is teetotally lying. Not a building down there is dilapidated. And the children bathe regular in tin tubs by the heater."

Being as he was so nasty about it, I said to him: "Well, you may live in this beautiful house on Boulevard, but all the same you is lying in your fancy gold teeth." Then he really went to rearing and pitching, and he said if I wasn't out his house in five minutes he'd have the law on me. And he said: "You'll pay for them children if you get them back. If they *is* your children." By this time he was on the porch and me and Maggie was on the street and we was still jawing back and forth right smart, and he was talking about the chain gang. He's dead now and I know he must be frying in hell, the old bastard.

Soon Walters sent me a letter saying I had to pay twenty-six dollars to get my children out the Masonic home. I got the money from a lady I had worked for one while, and I gave it to John D. and he went back to Americus in his truck with it. I phoned Mrs. Booker long distance and told her to get the children ready, John D. was on the way after them. John D. didn't have no trouble when he got there, and he brought them right on home with him.

I heard tell that later on Walters went down and investigated and found everything just like I told him, and they say they made the home better after that.

I couldn't stay on at Mrs. Warner's with two children, so here I went to moving again. We went back with Florrie and John D., and I got an old lady and paid her a dollar and a half a week to stay there and look after the children. We did that way until I could get us a place.

My cousin Veda was getting old, and she said she'd come to live with me and take care of the children while I worked. We got a place on Newman Street near Florrie, but bad times come at us. I came down with the flu—that's what folks went to calling the breakbone fever—jobs was hard to find, and I sure went to catching the devil every way. Everybody else was having a hard time too; there just wasn't no work to be found. I never was out of a job before except when I was down sick. Lose a job then on account of you were sick and you'd have to walk the streets looking for another one when you could get up again. It was enough to run us all crazy.

This woman I knew—I wouldn't say a friend of mine, but I knew her to speak to—got to talking to me one day and she said: "Why don't you go and get on the relief?" I didn't a bit more know what relief was than my house knew. This was in 1933 or '34, and this is where Mr. Roosevelt came in. I had heard all my days about poor folks getting on the city, but I hadn't heard about no relief. This woman told me about Mr. Roosevelt helping the poor folks, both colored and white, and she told me where the building was, down on Pryor Street. I couldn't hardly believe she meant it. She said: "Let me tell you what they do for me." And she said her husband was old and sick and not able to work and she couldn't work for taking care of him, which I knew for sure that much was right. She said: "They pay my rent and give us food. They even give us clothes and coal and wood." She said if I'd get on down to Pryor Street, a visitor would come out and investigate.

One cold day I hunted around and found where the office was. Meantime Veda had left me and gone to stay with somebody who could feed her better, which I couldn't fault her for that. I rented Veda's room to a woman; it was a dollar and a half a week, and she paid it when she had it. Me and her went that morning after I sent the children to school. The lady took our names and gave us a card, but we was there all day before we got wrote up, there was so many ahead of us. The lady said there'd be a visitor out to see us, so for me to stay right around the house. I felt better satisfied when she said a visitor would come, because we needed help bad. We was borrowing and living on the hands of other folks, and Lord it was awful. I know poor Dan was turning over in his grave.

When the visitor come I didn't ask for no rent, because I was renting that room. If you had any income at all you weren't supposed to ask for rent. The visitor said: "We don't usually give out relief immediately like this, but I'm going to do it today because I see how conditions are with you." And she gave me a relief check for eleven dollars and seventy cents right then. She advised me to shop at the chain stores to get food at lower prices, and I said I sure would do any way she said do.

After that I got seven-fifty a week and she had me sent out some coal and wood, and at the office they give me some slips to get clothes for me and the children. They'd give you these pieces of paper and you could go to any store—Rich's or Davison's or any place—and they'd take the slips from you instead of money. The relief gave me altogether eighteen or nineteen dollars in slips for our clothes. I spent my slip on Viola and Joyce because they needed shoes and raincoats and all to go to school. By going to school, they needed more than I did. I did get a piece of black material to make me a housedress.

After the visitor left that first time the people next door were just rearing to know. They were kindly backward and they were still scared of relief. This woman said the stores would give you spoiled food for your food slips, you could only get good food with money. Soon as the visitor left I went to the store, and that night we had the best supper we'd had for I don't know how long—cheese and eggs and hot rolls. That night we had plenty. This smart-alecky woman went to the store with me, and I made sure she saw the man cut my cheese off the same block as hers—and she had money.

Every week for way over a year my slips would come. Then they got it up to see who on relief was really able to work and who wasn't. So we all had to go and be examined by government doctors. And I mean they ever more than examined us, too. My eyes was bad and my teeth was worse. They said I had to get all my teeth taken out, and they said my health would improve if I saw about my teeth right away. I always was scared of a dentist so I didn't do that, but two or three that was hurting me I did have out.

They had said: "All who is able to work, we're going to put them to work. As soon as your papers come back we'll know, and we'll see you about work if you're able. If not, a nurse will come." In five or six weeks a nurse come to see me. My stomach and a knot in my side had been giving me down the country, and turned out I had to go to the Grady for local treatments. I went twice a week for a few weeks, and then it cleared up some and I went to going just once a week. They told me what to eat and what not to eat, and I did it for a while.

Then one morning I got a penny postal card saying to apply to the Pryor Street office, that I was able to go to work. I was so glad I jumped sky high. It was so good not to have to walk and walk and walk and hunt for the work. Strong and able-bodied women, they put them to work in the fields—in the parks is what it really was. Me and others they put in a sewing-room. I worked in the sewing-room at Morris Brown College and made seven-fifty a week. First I made pillow cases. We sewed everything by hand. You'd sew a little piece about an inch long, and if every stitch wasn't perfect that teacher would pull it every bit out. I know I was two months making Joyce a dress, because the teacher kept pulling it out until I got it perfect. That helped me a lot, and that's why I can sew so good today. When my eyes will let me, I can study out any kind of a pattern, and I can copy nearly anything I see without having a pattern; and if folks will hold still while I do the fitting, I can make a dress look like it grew on them. Later on they closed down the sewing-rooms, but the government employment-agencies would help folks get jobs in private homes and vouch for us.

Once the visitor asked me if I had insurance. So many people were dying without insurance, and then the burials would be on the government. I told her what I had, and it wasn't much. I had a whole flour sack full of old policies that I had paid on for years and had to let go because I wasn't able to keep them up. She looked through them and said: "Mmmmm—you sure have spent a fortune on policies." She said: "You take all these old policies down to 160 Pryor Street and somebody there will tell you which ones of these are any good now," and she gave me the name of the man to see.

Next morning I told Maggie about it and she said: "If you get messed up with that you'll get cut plumb off the government. If you can cash in these policies, you know they ain't going to give you no more food slips." Maggie always knew everything, even if sometimes she knew it all wrong. But this sounded quite natural—the visitor had thought I might get a hundred dollars or more for them policies.

I went on down though—with Maggie wringing her hands and hollering after me what a fool I was—and the man nearly died on the vine. "Good God Almighty!" he said. "You mean to tell me you been paying on all these policies?" I said not for a long time. He went to laying them out. All that was no good he dropped in the waste-basket, and when he got through wasn't but one kind out of the basket. That was the Metropolitan. Wasn't a one of them companies no good but the Metropolitan. All that other, he said, I might as well have throwed my money in the fire.

He said I ought to get around about a hundred and ninety dollars though. I don't rightly remember how it worked, but seemed like I had policies on nearly 'bout all my kinfolks—Florrie, Paul and Silas, David, Violet, J. W. Workman, Viola, Joyce, and me. I had the policies on them so if they died I could bury them. Each had to sign his own before I could cash it in. The ones in Atlanta I got signed and went back to Pryor Street with them in the next day or two. The man said it would be good and a month before I'd get the money. I went to counting every day. At that time I was still getting my seven-fifty a week for sewing.

One Saturday morning I saw something sticking out the mailbox, and, praise God, it was checks. Two had come, for nineteen dollars and fourteen dollars, on two of the policies. Florrie and Silas had to sign these checks before I could cash them. Florrie made me give her five dollars to sign hers, and I did because I didn't want no argument. And I was too happy to fuss. It was close to Easter-time and I'd been studying how I was going to get the children fixed up for Easter.

Next Monday morning here come two more checks. One was sixty dollars and the other was eleven or twelve. Every so often a couple more checks would come. After the last of them I figured it up and it was two hundred and two dollars. That's why I'm crazy about the Metropolitan.

Me and Maggie plumb fell out about this insurance. First she blessed me out and said I'd lose my sewing job, and she was stomp-down wrong about that for I worked for the relief a long time after all those checks come. Then Maggie wanted the sixty-dollar check to pay for her stove, which it was true they'd come to take it away from her twice already. I said I couldn't, and she said she'd pay me back two dollars a week. I knew I'd have been old as the Chattahoochee River before I got that sixty dollars back, and I said I was sorry but I wouldn't do it and BAM, the friendship ended like that. I'd have just been purely giving it to her. Maggie never paid back nobody. She always had so many debts on her she couldn't hardly pay folks back. Then too, I've known her to have money and she didn't pay her just debts then either.

Quite a while after, the government employment-place got me a good cook job. That's still going on and they don't charge you for it. You got to go a lot of times maybe, but they'll get you a job. Got to where things were pretty good again for jobs.

While we was on the sewing thing the visitor said: "I got good news for you. The government is going to put up nice homes for you all—either houses or apartments." When she went to talking about hot and cold water and heat, I didn't believe her.

I didn't hear much more about it for a right smart while. Then one day I asked a colored man on the bus and he said: "Oh yes, they building those houses on the West Side. They're nearly through. They call them government houses, and they're specially for folks on relief." Still and yet I rocked along and messed along and didn't go to see about it in time, so I didn't get one. Where I was then wasn't so bad or I guess I would have gone sooner.

But then somebody bought the house I lived in, and there we were all having to move. It was a bum place I got, too, just terrible, but I couldn't find anything else so I had to take it. It was in a big old rooming-house on Chestnut Street, made into four apartments. The apartment we was in had four rooms. Me and the two children had the front room; I sub-rented that from the people what rented the four-room apartment. Some of the rooms in that place had as many as four people in them. The back room was a long room, and six was staying in that one. And all of us had to use the same bathroom. Upstairs the same way. Those apartments were really meant for just one family. We figured it up, and one while there was eighteen of us using that one bathroom. The tub wasn't fit to use anyhow; it was black as the inside of a pocket. We tried and tried, but you couldn't get that thing scrubbed clean noway.

Everybody took turns cleaning the bathroom once a week, and we had a fuss about that. I said eighteen people using a bathroom, it should be cleaned every day; and the truth of the matter is it should have been cleaned twice or more a day. I do think that's what's the matter with Viola today. She cleans the bathroom all the time. Sometimes before breakfast, bless God, she's cleaning the bathroom, and she smells up the place with Chlorox and ammonia so it makes me sick. After we fell into that mess with eighteen people for that one bathroom, I was sure sorry I hadn't gone ahead and put in for one of those government houses, and I planned to be in time for the next set.

One Thursday when I was off I met a friend of mine up town. She lived in the first government houses that was built in Atlanta—that's the John Hope project—and I went home with her to look at it and hear about it. And when I saw and heard, I was disgusted with myself. Thursday, which it was my only day off, was a bad day to put in for one. There'd be so many people ahead of me I couldn't get waited on before the place closed. I lost three whole Thursdays that way. The lady I worked for told me they were going out of town soon and for me to wait until then and just take a day off and go out and put in for one. Me and Joyce went one morning. The girl wrote me up, and with that my application was in. She told me I'd have a visitor real soon, and about the second or third week the visitor come. I was at work, but Joyce was there and the visitor saw how we was living. She taken down how many people was in the building, and about the bathroom and all, and she said we sure did need a place.

She told Joyce she'd drop me a card when to come back to see them. I know I waited at least three or four months, and other people were just a-getting those places, and I got real worried. I sent Viola out there and the lady said they had done written us, and she said the date the letter was sent and everything, but I never got it. So I missed out on the John Egan houses.

I tried not to be too down in the mouth about it, and I went back and said: "Well, they're building another batch over on Edgewood and I'd like to get one of those." She said being as I'd had such a time getting one and she couldn't fault me for it, she'd put my application No. 2 on the list and she was sure I'd get a place real soon.

Every morning when I'd go to work the Bowers would ask me did I go out to the office about my apartment and I'd tell them what I'd did. Both of them acted like they wanted me to get it, but they were nasty people to start with. I found out later they fell out with everybody. Anyhow they did recommend me highly when the government phoned them to get my record—how much I was paid, how long I'd been with them, and things like that. The office man said very few stood that high with their people they worked for. He called Mrs. Anderson, that's who I was renting from, and she said she hated to lose me because I'd pay my room rent if we was hardly even eating.

One summer evening when I went home the children had gone to the show—some white lady had give them the money to go—and Florrie was sitting on the porch waiting for me. She said: "I come to see you about a house. Geneva is going to move in the project and I want you to take her house. I'm tired of coming down here, and I want you to get the children out of this old nasty slum-hole." I 'lowed I wasn't going to move back to Dunlap again, and she went to telling me how I'd never get in the project, long as I'd been waiting and still was. She almost got me downhearted then, but I said: "I will, too."

She went on home soon, and I went in the house and turned on the light. First thing I saw was a letter the children had put up on the mantelpiece. It was from the office for me to come to the house-opening on Sunday, and it said they had an apartment for me. I got so glad that my hat went one way and my shoes went the other. I sure laughed at Florrie, which of course she was done gone and it didn't do me no good. I went down the hall and showed the letter to Beulah, and it made her sick. Then I come on up and went to see good old Dora. Everybody I told—and I told everybody I could get at—was wishing it was them. When I got through phoning and running all over the building with my letter, I hotfooted it over to Florrie's, and I sure made Florrie read my letter. I all but rubbed her nose in it. Then she went to fussing at John D. because he hadn't put in for one. I left them jawing at each other and went back home, so I could be there to tell the children soon as they got in from the show.

Sunday couldn't come quick enough to suit me. I didn't have to go to work until late on Sundays, eight-thirty or nine, because the Bowers would go to Mass. Then they'd pick me up on the corner of Peachtree and Peachtree Battle Avenue. But that Sunday they sure got their breakfast before Mass, because I was in their house at quarter to seven with my tongue tied in the middle and wagging at both ends. I didn't know how would they take it, because you never could tell about them. Most usually she was the meanest woman ever put a shoe on her foot, but still she was nice in lots of ways. She'd cry a while and cuss a while, and I just didn't understand her. People didn't know how to figure her out, and he was just about as bad. This day she said she'd drive me over to the project for the meeting. That's how she was so peculiar; she'd do something nice for you, then turn right around and be hissing and spitting like a viper.

I hurried up and gave them such an early dinner they couldn't hardly eat it. She had done changed her mind about taking me to the auditorium, and she just drove me to the car line. I met the children and Beulah down on Edgewood and we come on down Fort Street to the project office. The auditorium was just packed. Everybody sang and prayed, and it was very nice. Then the manager, Hugh Thomas, got up and made a speech. He was a well-set-up light-brown man. He told us that all who had letters had needed a place urgently and all who had cards were on the waiting list. They went to grumbling, some of them, and he explained that quite naturally the ones that needed to move the worst were the ones that got the letters. "They had to be placed first," he said.

He told all us with letters a certain amount of money to bring the next day. If you put in for two rooms you brought a certain amount; and them who had put in for three, he told them how much more to bring. Those who put in for four had to bring nine dollars. That was me.

And I was sitting up there with three dollars in my hand. Beulah knew that was all I had and she laughed at me because she was jealous-hearted. I said I'd make sure to get up that nine dollars, but I mainly just said it to make Beulah hush her mouth.

I didn't sleep a bit that night, studying where could I get that rent. I thought I should get it right where I worked at. I knew it would be against her will for me to be off on a Monday, but I plain out had to do it. I got up soon Monday morning and walked that mile from the car line before the Bowers was out of bed. I told him I needed ten dollars, which I thought that was a big pile of money to be asking for, but he said it wasn't nothing and he'd gladly let me have it. I said I wouldn't move until my day off, Thursday, but I had to go back that very day to put up my money. They both nearly fell flat when I talked about leaving the house and it a Monday, and he said: "We going to lose friendship yet over those God damn projects." They both cussed more than anybody I ever seen excusing little Bradford. I used to tell them they ought to at least say damn instead of God damn, because God damn is cussing real bad.

Anyhow, she said she could understand about the meeting Sunday was just to explain things and why we'd need to go back Monday with the money. He said: "Hell, anybody can understand it, but all the same our housework has got to go undone on account of them." He meant the government, and he really was against the projects all along.

He finally said all right but they'd take it out of my pay, and he got right nasty. I didn't appreciate him saying that, because I had told them to take it out of my pay when I first brought it up.

When they come on down to breakfast she throwed the ten dollars on the work space where I was at. She said: "I wish you all the luck in the world, but if you can get back in time to fix dinner tonight I wish you would." I said I didn't really see how I could, I'd be pretty tired—walking two miles a day to and from the car line is no plaything. I told her just to take out of my pay for that whole day and not to count on me for dinner.

It was five-thirty when we left off the grounds at the project. We had done been there all day long, and some people didn't get waited on at all but had to go back the next day. I got my place all right though. Me and Viola picked out apartment No. 130. What made it so nice, you didn't have to take no pig in a poke. They give us each three cards, and you could pick from those three. Looked like a thousand people was there picking out apartments. Talk about camp-meeting day, this thing looked like that great gittin' up morning. You'd have to get one of the white-coated butlers who had the keys, and them butlers was cracking their coattails around all day.

No. 130 was the prettiest place you most ever seen. Nobody had even been inside there, which some of the places was all tracked up from people looking. There was a nice living-room, kitchen, refrigerator, two bedrooms, and everything brand-new and handy as a pocket in a shirt. I am crazy about a good-looking kitchen, and that kitchen was a dream. And on top of it all, a nice backyard where I could have a flower garden. Every house had one. A clothesline was already put up in each backyard, and a great big new garbage can. It was the same as heaven on earth to me. Viola and Joyce too, only they got it a heap sooner then me—Viola was sixteen then and Joyce fourteen.

Then there I was, had the apartment and nothing to put in it. After Dan died, I had sold the furniture all down to just a few things, a piece at a time when I needed the money. All I had left was a bedroom suit and two pieces of willow sun-parlor stuff for the living-room, two straight chairs, and a few dishes.

The old place had cost ten dollars a month and the project was sixteen. It was harder, quite naturally, to pay six dollars more but we just strained up and did it. And I did go right to buying things on time. First I got a breakfast suit, because I didn't have a thing for the kitchen. The next thing was two little linoleum rugs for the kitchen and the living-room. Then I didn't buy anything else until I paid for the rugs and most of the breakfast-room suit. All three of us was still sleeping in the same room because all I had was the two twin beds. I used to purely hate to go home at night and look at that other nice bedroom with nothing in it. I kept wanting furniture for it, but couldn't see my way into it for a right smart while. Then one morning I was looking in the paper and saw an ad for a nothing-down furniture sale and I said: "Well, this is my day." I bought me a bed and a mattress and two pillows. It was a four-post mahogany bed and it looked mighty good, but it wasn't worth two cents. The slats were always falling down, and many a night I just went on sleeping half way betwixt the bed and the floor.

The first night we spent in the project didn't nobody get any sleep at all, and not for some time after. Everybody was so glad and rejoicing for them nice homes that they couldn't rest. People would just spend the night walking around their own apartments, looking. Any time of night, you could look through their windows—the shades weren't drawn, either they didn't have any yet, and wasn't nothing to hinder you from seeing—and there they'd be, just walking round and round their apartments and looking up at the ceilings. I know that's what they were doing because I asked a woman one morning on my way to work. She said the ceilings were so good, which most of them never slept under a stout ceiling in all their born lives before, and she said they was so rejoicing and proud. I said: "Well, honey, that's a poor way to feel, to be proud over it. You ought to just get down on your knees and thank God and President Roosevelt."

Mr. Bower had been telling me all the time to rent one of the bedrooms, which of course that was directly against the project rules and still is and he knew it. After he had kept on at me about it though, it turned out Odessa Cartwright had to move and she was just as good as outdoors; so I taken her in, her and her husband. They were Cartwrights, but not a bit of kin to me. They said if I'd take them in they'd pay half the rent, and Mr. Bower said: "Do it and keep your mouth shut. It's nobody's business but your own."

We were doing pretty well. Joyce had got dissatisfied with us going along so slow, and she had quit school in the ninth grade so she could help. She got a little afternoon job pressing clothes and such for some lady. She got five dollars a week and carfare, and that helped us some. Viola was making seven a week. So we rocked along and everything was going nicely—Joyce and Viola both working, and Odessa and Rob paying half the rent.

I wasn't noways particular about the Bowers, but what really got my goat was the ritzy way they had me to serve meals. Which it didn't do them a bit of good anyhow to put on a show for company, not the way they was behaving. Mr. Bower had hated me ever since I got into the project, and he just got nastier and nastier—and he had a running start on being nasty to begin with. One night they was having company and I was serving dinner and he was telling the man about the project, right in my face. "You ought to be rich like my maid here," he said. "She's got a refrigerator big enough for an elephant to have a baby in. I carried her home the other night so I could take a look at her place, and there sat this big damn refrigerator bigger than mine. But you know what she had in it? Not one God damn thing but a bar of P & G soap!"

Well, when he said that, it really got me bad. That hurt me. Why, I never used P & G soap in my life; it was a package of margarine he seen. I told him that, right while I was serving to the left and taking off at the right. Then Mrs. Bower mixed in. She said: "Willie Mae, that's what I dislike about you. Whenever Mr. Bower says anything you don't like, you stop whatever you're doing and try to straighten him out." Which I wasn't stopping at all, I kept right on with that serving to the left and taking off at the right while I told him. I guess the company thought didn't none of us have any manners. And every time I'd come back in the dining-room, Mr. Bower would start on it again. He told the man: "Hell, we never will be able to have nothing ourselves no more. Paying all these high taxes for refrigerators for people like Willie Mae. That's what's keeping us down. That damn man in the White House is going to ruin us all."

My vacation was coming up in June. I had always got a week off with pay, but this year I was broke-down tired and I asked for a second week without pay. I dreaded to ask her, because there never was no way to know how was the right way to say a thing to her. You'd try to handle her like she was made of tissue paper, but even that didn't do no good if she was just ripe to do you dirty. Happen she was in one of her good spells though, and she said I'd be welcome to a second week without pay. She wasn't never in a good spell with her poor mother though. It was pitiful the way she was always so nasty to her mother. That night we fixed it up for me to be off two weeks, her mother cried and said I was her best friend and she hated to see me go. She was a real old lady.

Mrs. Bower owed me nine dollars and the week off with pay made it eighteen, which she didn't give me but twelve dollars because she didn't have it all right then. She would have given me a check for the whole thing, but I didn't want a check because it's hard for a lot of us colored folks to get a check cashed. I have to go where I'm known to get a check cashed—to my insurance company, the drug store where I get my medicine at, or the furniture store, and none of those places is handy to where I live. The curb market is near, but it's so big that I'm not known to anybody there.

Mrs. Bower used to send me to Davison's a lot to buy stockings for her, so they did know me there, and she said she'd take the six dollars and leave it for me at the stocking counter. I did without it all that week. Next week on a Tuesday morning I phoned her, and that's when the mess come off. I asked her if she'd please leave my money at the stocking counter that day and she said: "What money?" I told her, which of course she already knew it, how my pay lacked six dollars. She said she didn't know what I was talking about, and at first I thought she was kidding— sometimes she did used to go on a lot of foolishness—but she wasn't. She said: "All I want to hear out of you is when you're coming back to work," and she talked real short and hateful. I said I had used to know when I was coming back but now I didn't, because I didn't want to come back if she didn't pay me my six dollars. At that, she banged up the receiver.

When I had left for my vacation, Mrs. Bower's sister had loaned me her radio to bring home with me because I didn't have one. Mrs. Bower must have told Mrs. Coates about what happened between us on the phone, because Mrs. Coates called and asked me to bring back the radio. Wanted it right away, she said; and if I didn't bring it right away she'd send after it. Next day here come one of the building service men just a-running, with a message for me to come to the office "on some very personal business."

He said: "Don't give me away, I'm not supposed to tell you this, but these people you been working for are mad with you. She called up over to the office, and she low-rated you like a dog. She's begging them to put you out of the project. She told them you were renting a room, won't work, drink rot-gut whisky every night, run a dissipated house, and every other Lord's thing she can think of." It made me sick.

Odessa was at the store, and when she come back I told her. She had just sent Rob to get another suitcase of clothes, and she like to broke her neck stopping him from bringing anything else in the house. Odessa's husband's son Jake worked at the project, and happen he come by when me and Odessa was sitting there studying what could we do. He said: "I know exactly who in the office would write up that complaint. She's a personal friend of mine, and so is the manager. I'll see both of them for you before you go to the office."

I was so nervous I didn't know what to do. Next morning I had the worst spell I ever had in my life and I had to call the doctor, and that's something I don't do in any hurry. Four dollars a call, and sometimes they don't even take your temperature. I know I was in such a fix because I was so sure I'd lost my apartment. Looked to me like my heart was going to come right out of my mouth. The doctor told me not to get out of the bed, I was in a bad shape. He called it something I can't remember, but I was ever more than sick.

Mrs. Coates come over that night to get her radio. She came with her boyfriend. He was a doctor, but he just stayed in the car even after she seen how sick I was. She picked up her radio and went on out the door, and she still had in her hand the money she had brought in. I thought it was my six dollars Mrs. Bower owed me. I reckon if I'd said I'd be back to work the next day or so she'd have handed me the money; we saw the paper money folded in her hand when she came in. I'd been with the Bowers nearly nine years, sometimes working day and night, but that's how it ended.

The girl in the office who did the writing up come down home to see me. She said she didn't know I was sick or she wouldn't have told me to come to the office. I told her I hadn't got sick till she told me to come to the office. My doctor had said that the shock of the trouble with the Bowers had hastened on my sickness, although I would have had it some time anyhow. This girl said Rob had explained things to her and she hadn't even carried the complaint to the manager. She showed me exactly what she had written down, and she sure did have a beautiful handwriting.

It was true I was breaking the rules taking in roomers, but it shows if God's for you the devil can't harm you. This girl said for me to come up when I was able and explain how come Odessa and Rob was there. She said: "Mr. Thomas ain't going to throw you outdoors when he understands how it came about. He's very nice. But you ought to tell him. You just go and explain the whole thing to him." And she made an appointment with him for the end of the week.

Me and Odessa comes on up to the office on that day. Mr. Thomas was sitting up there all reared back in his armchair, a great big rich-looking man, and I was sure scared. I didn't know how to start telling him, because I knowed I was in the wrong. Soon as I could untangle my tongue I said: "I have did something against the project rules, and I want to tell you about it my own self. I'd have been here before, but I been sick. These people been living with me. They had to get out of where they was, and they had nowhere to go to. They're real old people, and in times past they helped me in this same way." This was gospel truth, but I didn't tell him I needed them too to help pay the rent.

Mr. Thomas didn't even spend no time studying about it. He said: "If they sheltered you, this is no more than what you should do for them now. Rules is rules, but people is people, too. For the time being you let them stay right where they are, and just don't go blabbing it all over the project."

Wasn't no need to go blabbing; everybody knew about it anyhow. So much as let your stomach growl and everybody knew it just as good as if you'd put a notice in the morning *Constitution*. One day Mr. Thomas come to my place to see Rob, and everybody was throwing doors open all up and down the court. They just knew he had come to put me out, and they aimed to see it happen. I had a fine time laughing at them, since this was just a friendly visit to Odessa's husband. Rob went to work and just put Mr. Thomas right up on the top shelf. He said: "Thomas, I'm so proud of you with this fine government job, managing all these people and all these houses." He laid it on so thick he needed a trowel, still and yet he did mean it. Me and Odessa fixed Mr. Thomas some coffee, and we sure kept pushing it to him.

We was all straightened out then, and we went to living like folks. Odessa and Rob stayed with us eight months before they got a place, and Mr. Thomas never said one other word to us about it.

*   *   *

But them Bowers wasn't through with me yet. I was stretching curtains one day, and here come Essie over from her side of the project. She was Mrs. Bower's friend's maid, and, by Mrs. Bower putting her up to it, she was always snooping around to see had I done been thrown out. She scared me pea green and popeyed when she told me Mrs. Bower had gone over the manager's head and gone to see the people at the project headquarters in the First National Bank Building. When they asked Thomas, Lord love him for a cheerful liar, he told them it wasn't a word of truth in what Mrs. Bower had told on me.

Next thing, I got a slip to come to 160 Pryor Street, the relief office. It was a Mr. Church I seen there and, when he asked me what was going on, I just bleated out the whole thing. Looked like to me he was embarrassed over the way them Bowers had done me. Before you could say Withlacoochee, he had give me carfare to go see his wife and I got one of the best cook jobs I nearly ever had.

I stayed with the Churches for nearly two years, and it was them that got me out of eating starch. I had got the habit when we was in all that mess in Adel—with Fred cutting the fool and not earning a living, and Babe trying to feed us all and not able to. If you eat starch, you don't be hungry for anything else much. I had eat it some before, but that time in Adel was when I got the habit bad.

The Churches nearly 'bout had a fit when they seen what I was doing. I'd just set my little box of Argo starch down at one end of the ironing-board, and eat it a pinch at the time all the while I was ironing. And then I wouldn't want no lunch. That was how they come to notice. At that time I wasn't eating much starch anyhow, never more than three boxes a day; but they give me a big bottleful of these vitamin pills, and I took them and got out of the habit altogether, and I been eating like a field hand ever since.

Plenty of folks around the project eat starch though. Clay too. It's a man lives out Decatur Street a piece, and he comes to the project regular twice a week selling clay— real fine white clay—in little paper sacks, ten cents a sack. I never cared for clay ever, just starch. And I don't believe this white clay is a bit better than plain old clay anyhow, but lots of folks buy it from him. The Churches like to died when I told them about that.

After I stayed with them the biggest portion of two years, the government transferred him to New York. I told Essie they were leaving Atlanta, and she raced right to the Bowers to tell them. Mrs. Bower said she was glad and she hoped I'd be out of a job.

I all but was out of a job, too. I went to doing day work, two and three hours each place. It had got bad again about jobs, and I was just picking here and there doing the best I could. Then Hartley, a friend of mine in the basement at the Pershing Point Apartments, told me there was a lady there from Washington wanted somebody to work. So I went on out Peachtree to see her. She was Mrs. Clifford.

When I got there, Mr. Bob had the piano all tore up and

was working on it, and they both had on shorts—his was bright yellow and hers bright blue. They looked mighty curious to me. I had never seen anybody look like that. Wearing bright-colored shorts around the house, and she looks different anyhow. She wasn't really pretty maybe, but she had such cute ways you always thought she was. Her skin was reddish brown and her hair was long and yellow and all hanging down, and all I know to say is that she looked sort of foreign looking. He had those pretty blue eyes, but they always looked like he was sleepy.

I said to myself: "Oh, Lord, I ain't going to like it here. These is show folks, and I don't want to work for them." And then what capped it all was when she told me to make them a highball. I never worked for nobody what told me to make them a highball. She told me to put one jigger of whisky and two of that White Rock water. When I went to mixing it, I thought she must have said two of the whisky and one of the water because it didn't look like one of the whisky would have been enough. I never had mixed a drink before in my life and I didn't know.

They set back with their drinks, and I went on back in the kitchen. He come in there later, about half high by that time, and asked me what my name was again. He kept calling me Lily Mae until he got the straight of it. Then he said: "Willie Mae, we sure do like you. You're going to be our girl. You can work for us all your life." I said: "Yes, sir," but I was saying in my mind that I knew I wasn't, because I just didn't want no truck with them.

Then she come in the kitchen, saying how good the highballs was, and to fix him another one. She was getting high too, and just laughing and talking. I made him another one, and after he downed that he was high as a Georgia pine. When he finished it he come in the kitchen again and give me a dollar, and I knowed then that Katie had done barred the door; I knowed he was drunk then.

They were laying back in their chairs and talking, and they asked me how many children I had. I told them two. They wanted to know what their names were, and I told them Joyce and Viola. I never had worked for anybody asked all these kind of questions about me, and I said to myself: "These ain't a thing but old show folks. Asking all these questions, and tight as Dick's hatband anyway." Course after he give me the dollar, I begin to say to myself that they might do very well.

I went on downstairs in the basement and the boy what got me the job was down there—he was the porter. He asked me how I was liking it and I said: "Well, Hart, I'm going to tell you the truth. I don't think I'm going to like them." He wanted to know why, and I said I never worked for anybody asked me to make a highball and that I didn't want to fool with anybody like that. Hart said: "Oh, that's all right, Willie Mae. They're good folks." I didn't tell him I thought they was show folks, because I was afraid he might let it slip what was on my mind.

When I went home that day, I told all the neighbors I didn't know if I was going back there to work or no. I told them all how the Cliffords looked and everything, and they all said yes the Cliffords must be show folks. Two folks I don't want nothing to do with is show folks and gypsies. I wouldn't trust them behind a broomstraw.

When the day come for me to go back to the Cliffords, I got to thinking. I said: "Well, the pay's better than I been getting and they were nice, so I'll go back and try again. But if they got on those short breeches and tell me to go to making highballs again, I don't think I'll stay."

When I went back, he wasn't there—which was much better, because that way I didn't have to be bothered about no highballs. She was straightening up the apartment, and she had on a sweet little dress. I was a little bit late. I didn't want to go, and I fooled around at home, and when I got there I was late. I was hot and tired too, but I said I was sorry I was late. She said: "Oh, that's all right. We got plenty of time. Just so you get here, it's all right." That made me feel so good I said to myself: "Oh-oh. These my folks after all, I believe."

Later she went to telling me what was in the refrigerator and what to fix for lunch. She said: "We can have either Coca-Cola or tea, and fix me a plate too and we'll have lunch together." I said to myself: "Oh, sweet Jesus, I know I'm on a spot now. Now I know they's show folks." But I just said all right ma'am and I went on ahead and fixed it.

Me and her sit down for lunch, and that was the first time I ever had a job that the woman did that. So we set there and ate lunch and talked, but I was worried in mind.

I seed she was good, yet and still I thought she might be going to get me hung up and then go off and leave me without my pay. I thought she might be baiting me in, and some day I'd go there and they'd have slipped out and gone.

But I just worked along, and some days she'd be there and some days she wouldn't. I never did ask her what broadcasting station they worked at or where they played or acted at. I just knew they were show folks though, because she had all those wide curious hats, and she wore different things from other folks, and she just didn't look right to me. Right ain't in it though; come to be they were the best people on earth and can't be matched up anywhere.

When I got acquainted with her good, we sit down at the table one day just talking. She went to telling me how well she liked me. She said: "I thought I liked Leila in Washington, but I like you a damn sight better." She said: "Right when you first come, I said: 'Bob, that's my gal.' And he said so too." Then I said: "Well now I'll tell you what I said about you all." She said she wouldn't get mad, so I told her I had made sure they was show folks; the way they acted I had figured it out that he played the piano and she sang and danced. She just laughed and laughed. She said if she'd known, she'd have played the piano and had him going through some kind of foolishness the next time I came. I said if she had, I'd have gone right back out the door.

They were just so nice. At night he'd come in the kitchen, just as sober as I was. Every evening when he'd come in from work he'd always chat with me a while. He'd ask me how was my children and all such as that. He asked me once if I'd ever been up the country, and I said no. He said he knew 'most that some day they'd go back to Washington, and if I stayed with them he'd sure see that I got to Washington. That just thrilled me to death.

He was sure kind. In the evening when he'd come in the kitchen he'd be mixing highballs whilst he talked with me. He'd take them out to the living-room and later when I'd take the tray out to the kitchen, there'd be fifty cents on it, sometimes a dollar. By that extra money they give me, and the good salary, it made me get straightened out. It helped me a lot.

Soon after I got in with them, my money went to rolling. He worked at the Bell Bomber Plant at Marietta, and he had to entertain all them big men from up the country. They moved out on the Marietta Highway. I was working three days a week regular for them, and then he'd call me in on extra days when men from Washington and New York and Buffalo would come down to the plant.

I'd go out and cook supper for them, and sometimes I'd go to Buckhead in a cab and buy all the groceries. Sometimes I'd buy two fryers and I'd make rolls, and Mr. Bob was crazy about apple pie and cheese. He loved that better than a hog loves corn. He wouldn't forget his fifth, either;

he'd bring that with him. So I wouldn't have to buy any whisky.

I'd get out to the house early, and time they'd come I'd have everything looking pretty. She was working at Bell too, and she didn't have no time to do all this herself. I'd set the table so pretty, and put out her big monogrammed napkins, and then she'd go down in the woods and come back and mess up the table with pine needles. He used to say: "Lord, Willie Mae, I sure am glad you know how to cook." I was glad too, because it made them want to keep me on. He'd be getting high, but he'd come back and make his own drinks. They never did ask me to make no high-balls after that first day. I know they didn't like the ones I made, because they never did ask me to make no more. He'd fix all the highballs, even when they had company.

They'd all be in there eating and drinking, and plenty of nights I didn't leave until nine or nine-thirty. They'd ride me all the way home on those nights. One night I made seven dollars. Mr. Bob paid me five, and the two men gave me a dollar apiece because they said it was such a good dinner.

That kept going on so much till one day Miss Fay said: "Willie Mae, while you're making this good money you ought to go and see about your furniture."

Before I worked for the Cliffords, my place was nearly as naked as a newborn baby. It was so naked, when you talked it sounded hollow. I didn't buy any furniture then, because I wasn't particular about getting in debt. I knew I was going to pay the rent, and I wouldn't do anything else until I could see how I could.

I was scared to buy even after I was with the Cliffords. I was scared that time I got the furniture half paid for they'd be leaving for Washington and I'd be hung up with all that debt. This day though she said she'd guarantee they wouldn't leave before I got it paid for, and he said even if they did I wouldn't stand to lose either my money or the furniture. He said: "In that case I'd lend you the money to finish paying for it." He was cold sober, and he wasn't kidding.

So I went to looking around different furniture stores, seeing what I wanted to get. When I run up on a living-room suit I liked, I told Miss Fay. She had told me not to buy nothing second-handed and maybe have it fall to pieces on me. She said: "Buy you something new and something that'll hold up." So one day I met her downtown and took her by the store, and the whole suit was sitting in the window. It was heavy, good furniture, and she said I couldn't have done no better, and I was satisfied then.

When I got the down payment finished out, the store sent the furniture out home on one Saturday morning. Talk about making them sick around the project, they were a sight in this world that day. I don't know how many crowded up and watched the men bring it in. One man said it was the swellest living-room suit in the whole project, and I said: "That's why I bought it."

There was a white lady wanted that suit mighty bad. It stayed on in the window until I finished that big down payment, and one day she come in and wanted to buy it. She was there a day I was making a payment and she told me if I'd let her have it she'd pay me my money in it and ten dollars over. But I wanted it my own self and I wouldn't do it.

She was so vexed she whirled around and went over to the manager and one while I heard her say: "I didn't know you sold colored folks that kind of furniture." He said: "We's in business to sell furniture. Anybody with the money can buy anything we got." I told Miss Fay, and she said it wouldn't have done if she'd been down there and heard that white lady talk like that. I was glad she hadn't been there, because I knew Miss Fay would have blowed her sky high.

I wouldn't have had a stick of that furniture if I hadn't been with the Cliffords. It was right funny. I wouldn't buy nothing until I'd tell her. I'd say: "How much longer you all going to be here? Long enough for me to buy a rug?" She helped me get that odd square and lots of other things. She was always telling me: "Willie Mae, now you pay for your furniture as fast as you can, so you'll have it paid for when we leave here." I did, and the way it happened, I finished paying one month and they left for Washington the next month. That sure was knocking about.

Lots of times they'd ask me if I needed any money, and sometimes I'd be so worried my heart would be between my toes, but I wouldn't say so. I'd tell him I had some money and he'd say: "Let me see in your pocketbook. I believe you need some money." I'd say: "Oh, I ain't broke. I got fifty or seventy-five cents in my bag." And he'd say: "Well, take this dollar anyhow." That's the kind of folks they was, and that's how come I love them.

One night I dreamed about them. I dreamed they was separated. Soon as I saw her I told her, and I said: "Looked like to me I could just see somebody pushing you apart." She said that wasn't the way it was but that something had done happened. She told me he had got a dirty deal where he worked and they were going to Washington.

After they went to Washington, I went up there twice to see them. And not a Christmas passes but that I don't get a nice present from them—sometimes money, sometimes something pretty to wear. She writes to me sometimes, but not much. More often she sends me beautiful boxes of clothes. Other things, too. Once she sent me three table mats with pictures of Mt. Vernon, the Capitol, and the White House.

One Christmas I thought: "Well, I'm going to fix her this time. I'm going to show her I appreciate all they done for me." And I bought her a $5.98 slip with lace clean down to here, and I went to George Muse and bought Mr. Bob two pocket handkerchiefs for a dollar apiece.

I always tell them if they ever get down sick or Mr. Bob gets down on his luck so they can't have a maid—and lots of big shots has had that to happen—I'd come to them. I'd leave here walking if I had to, and go there and work and never look for no salary. They sure did give me my start. They give me luck.

Miss Fay said she wouldn't leave for Washington until she placed me in a good job, and she gave me to one of her friends and said that's the one she thought I ought to work for. I didn't work for her but one day, so I can't remember her name. But I can think of plenty of things to call her.

I was to work for her two days a week, and I had some other places for day work. She met me in Buckhead and when I got in the little car with her there wasn't hardly room for me to sit, she was so big and fat. We got out there, and, Lord have mercy, I was disgusted. I know she hadn't cleaned up that house in three months. She had used dishes, and when the sink got full she'd put them back up on the shelf, glasses milk had been in and everything.

I couldn't hardly work for knocking the roaches off. I put a heap of dishes to soaking and went to cleaning the house. I got nearly all the dishes done then, but some of the pans were so caked up with food I had to let them soak some more. Then she told me it was her little girl's birthday and she wanted a nice dinner for the child. She said she wanted fried chicken, light rolls, stewed corn, fresh butter beans, and boiled okra. She asked me if I wanted to make a cake or her to buy one, and I said I was so tired already I'd rather she'd buy one, so she did.

When I got all this big dinner cooked and ready, she kept holding back from putting it on the table. The child kept saying: "Come on, let's eat. I'm hungry." But her mother kept saying: "Just wait a while. I'm looking for a special little plate." I didn't know what was she talking about and neither did the child. Her mother said: "You know, Patsy's plate." Patsy was the dog. "Oh, I know," she said. "It's out on the porch." And she went and got it and brought it in to me. She was smiling sort of silly and just a-talking away. She said: "My other girl was crazy about that plate. She never wanted to eat out of anything but that plate, so I thought it'd be nice for you to do that way too."

I said: "Don't worry about that plate or any other dishes either. I'm not hungry anyhow." One minute there I thought I'd eat a chicken wing or a roll to save my stomach, but then I couldn't. If I was too dirty or germy to eat out of her dishes, I couldn't see how come I wasn't too dirty or germy to fix her food and put it in dishes for them to eat. I never before or since had anybody I worked for do that to me. I didn't say any of this to her though; I just told her I couldn't eat because I was sick at my stomach, which I was sick at my stomach just thinking about her and her mean ways.

I wouldn't noways have minded using a dish her dog

had eat out of. I never had separate dishes for any pet of my own, and some of the persnickitiest white folks I ever worked for never had separate dishes for their dogs and cats either. But this backward heifer didn't know no better—she thought it was dirty to use the same dish a dog had done eat out of, but still and yet she thought that was good enough for me.

When I left out of there late that afternoon she said she'd meet me at the car line in Buckhead the next day at eight in the morning, and I said: "Yes'm, I'll be right there at Miller's filling-station." I let her drive that whole eight miles the next morning; and if I was there, Mrs. Joe Louis was there.

For a while then I did day work around, and the children was both working, and all us brought in enough to get along with. One day I come home from a day job and found a telegram in the door: "Call me tonight at eight. Fay Clifford." I couldn't hardly wait until eight o'clock. Then when I did talk to her and heard what she wanted me for, I jumped up and cut a caper, rheumatism or no.

She had recommended me for a month's cook job with somebody in Washington. Really it was out from Washington a piece, in Maryland. This Mrs. Woodson's son was going overseas with the Army, and she wanted somebody up there to fix everything nice for him. I went on up there and she had people coming in all the time, lots of entertaining for her to do, and she did need me to cook.

One Sunday afternoon they had a buffet supper. They were crazy about Southern-fried chicken and hot light rolls. I don't know what all other things we didn't have. There was two or three different kinds of salad—tomato aspic and pineapple salad in ring molds—sweet lady peas, and every other thing. I started making rolls about one-thirty in the afternoon, and I fried around fifteen or sixteen chickens, just a pile of them.

Late in the afternoon the guests come—lots of big shots. Some from Maryland, some from Washington, and all other places around. I didn't know the Roosevelts were coming until I saw her already there. I asked one of the other maids who was that lady in the butler's pantry just now getting herself a drink of water, and she said: "That's the President's wife. Mrs. Roosevelt." I just laid down the rolls I was buttering and went straight to the dining-room door and looked all around for her.

Mrs. Woodson came over to see what I wanted—which of course I did want to ask her something—and I told her the maid said Mrs. Roosevelt was there and I wanted to know.

Miss Fay came over then too, and she was high as a Georgia pine, and they both said: "You don't need to worry. You're going to see both of them."

A little bit later they came and said: "Willie Mae, come on out to the car and meet the President."

He didn't come in; he just sit in the car. We went out

with a cup of tea. I was so nervous there was more in the saucer than in the cup by the time he got it. When I got out to the car, one of them—Miss Fay or either Mrs. Woodson, I don't remember which—spoke to him and said: "We're bringing somebody that wants to see you. This is Willie Mae from Georgia."

He said: "Why, hello, Willie Mae," and that voice sounded just exactly the way it did on the radio. It wasn't deep and boomy like some men's voices. It was higher than that, yet and still it was rich, and it was clear as could be. If I'd been a fish in the sea and that voice asked me did I want to come out on the land, I know I'd have come flipping right on out.

He taken my hand and asked me how I was. I told him I was feeling all right. He said: "You're from Georgia?" and I told him I was. He said: "What do your people in Georgia think of me?" I didn't know who was he talking about, my folks I work for or either my friends, so I told him, I said: "Everybody I work for, they all like you fine." (There was just one man I worked for that hated him, but I wouldn't have hurted the President's feelings for *that* man—he was the sorriest man God ever strung a gut to. Which of course President Roosevelt already knew there was plenty of people didn't like him, but I wouldn't have told him about this one for anything.) "For myself and my children and my friends," I said, "we're just crazy about you. We all love you."

He just looked at me and smiled. Miss Fay poked at me

and said to tell him why we loved him so. So I said: "Well, why we're so crazy about you is because of those nice projects you built. Well, I don't mean you built them, but you're the cause of them being built. Before we had a place in the project, the house we was living in, I could lay in the bed and look up and see the buzzards and birds and hawks flying, and in bad weather just as much rain would come in on my face as would be outdoors. Now we got a nice place to live: hot and cold water, plenty of heat, nice bedrooms and bath, and everything nice and convenient."

He asked me who was in my family and what size apartment we had, and I went to preaching some more about how fine the project was. All that time he was just a-holding my hand. The other men in the car were falling out laughing, but not him. He was looking me right square in the face and smiling real sweet. I told him, I said: "I'm living better now than I ever lived in my life." He still smiled and he still helt my hand, and he said he was so glad to hear me say that. I was so nervous till I sweated clear down to the bottom of my feet. I was so nervous because I had holt of the President's hand. If he'd of let me go I'd have felt better satisfied. It felt like to me the Lord had holt of my hand.

When I got back inside, I saw her. After I'd talked to him I wasn't noways afraid of her, so I went right in and looked for her. Happen I caught her in the butler's pantry again, getting another drink of water. I said: "Is this Mrs.

Roosevelt?" She said: "Yes, yes," quick like and friendly.
I said: "Well, I just been out there talking to your hus-
band." She said that was fine, and then I told her I was
Willie Mae and I was from Atlanta.

She asked me was I in Atlanta the time they come
through. I told her yes'm. "I was on the corner of Peachtree and Baker," I said, "and I didn't get a chance to see
you good, but I got a glimpse of you."

I told her how we all loved her husband for getting us
such good houses and jobs, and looked like that tickled her
to death. I told her I was working in Washington for a
month. She didn't ask me how much was I making, but I
up and told her. I said: "I'm making twenty-five dollars a
week and a round-trip ticket on the Streamliner." She
laughed and patted me on the shoulder. "That's very good,"
she said, and she did look to be real pleased over it.

She was a big, well-set-up woman. She wasn't so pretty,
but she was just so, I don't know, so sweet and kind; and
that dress she had on—it wasn't in the book. It was beautiful—black lace, and a great big bow (or maybe it was a
flower, I was so excited I couldn't look at her dress too
good) laying somewhere near her waist.

She went on back to mix and mangle with the party, and
I went back to my work. None of the other maids got to
see them, didn't nobody go but me. I was the biggest shot
in the kitchen. The reason was I was in Washington on a
visit, and Mrs. Woodson wanted me to see everything that
was exciting, and that's why I got to see the Roosevelts.

Me and Mrs. Woodson stayed up real late that night, getting things put away. I told her about how proud I was to be there with her and on top of everything getting to talk to the President. When I was talking to him, that smile and that voice was all I could think of; but after I come back in the house I remembered how sleepy and sad he looked. He had that smile all right, yet and still he looked sad, and he had big bags under his eyes. I told Mrs. Woodson and she said: "Willie Mae, he'll never live this term out." And sure enough, he didn't. Round about three weeks later, he died that Thursday.

When I come back to Atlanta from Washington, I told all the neighbors what a nice time I had. One old hateful somebody said: "I reckon you got to see the President too, didn't you?" I said: "See him! I shuck hands with him!" She like to dropped in her tracks, but soon she put on out and called everybody from all up and down the court to come and hear about my trip. And I made them sick.

I told them about a lots of the things I did and places Miss Fay took me. "And this is the wonderfullest thing that ever happened to me," I told them. "I have did something you never did." I said: "All you men what have been overseas and rode on boats—which I've been on a boat myself, years and years ago—and been up in planes: I have did something more important than all that. I have shaken hands with President Roosevelt."

Their tongues commenced to running then. I said: "Yes, I met him, and I shuck his hand, and I talked with him, and I carried him a cup of tea, and I preached a fair sermon out in front of his car." I kept excited about it and for a right smart while afterward when I'd go to bed at night sometimes I'd lay there and say to myself: "Willie Mae, you sure have been knocking about."

After that I had to hunt me some work, because I had quit all my day jobs to go to Washington. I got a cook job out in Druid Hills, five and a half days a week. And before I could bat my eyes, Joyce had married somebody wasn't worth a cuss.

She was about twenty then. Martin had a job singing at the picture show where she used to go after work with other girls from the laundry. He sang two nights a week. First time she made me acquainted with him I said to myself: "I don't like that fellow at all." He had all his hair carried back on his head and he just looked sorry to me. I knew he wasn't worth a dime as a worker; I could tell he didn't want to get his hands dirty.

Him and Joyce went together three or four months, then one day here he come bringing me ice cream. I had an idea what he was about, so I said real snappish to him: "Just put it in the refrigerator and you all can eat it later. I don't like ice cream myself." He went on ahead though and asked me what did I think about him and Joyce getting married. I knew he couldn't take care of a wife—him scared to get his hands dirty with work, and depending on his father except for what little he got paid for singing two nights a week. I know he figured Joyce would work and he'd get on fine. I told him Joyce could do to suit herself, but that I sure wouldn't marry anybody as sorry as he was. Soon after that he left, and he didn't come back to help eat his ice cream.

When I came home one evening, Viola said Joyce and Martin had gone over to the courthouse and got married that morning. Joyce and Martin was there in the apartment, but Viola met me at the door and told me. I talked to them very nice, but I wasn't happy in my heart about it. No need to be happy about it either, because it come to pass they wasn't married two months. Joyce soon seen he wasn't going to do no work, and she come on back to me. He had been stealing money out of her pocketbook and such as that, and she got so mad with him she didn't even feel bad about leaving him. She hauled right off and got a divorce.

After her divorce she started again to going with Gerald Stone. She'd been going with him before Martin even. Before he went in the Army in 1941 or 1942 he used to be our paper boy, and they started going together after he got out of the Army. In about three months they got married.

Gerald loved me because I was nice to him. He had lost his mother, and he didn't get along with the aunt he lived with. When he told me him and Joyce were going to get married, I said: "Well, just go to it, and I hope she'll do better this trip than she did before." I liked Gerald and I would have been nicer to him but they were both so young, and I wasn't particular about her marrying anybody again in such a hurry. I knowed Joyce was so mean and quick-tempered that I didn't know how they'd get along, and I didn't want her to keep marrying and jumping from one to another.

Gerald was a nice boy though, and he was real tired of Army life and wanted to get a little home and settle down. They went to live with this old aunt of his, but she was so crabbish and hateful they couldn't stay. They went out on the West Side and got them a little house out there. First they rented, then they bought this home in Dixie Hills. That development was just new built up then, and they got a nice little place.

It came about that Joyce and Gerald did real well. Onli-est thing what made me uneasy about Gerald oftentimes was he'd get so riled up about not being able to get good jobs or go certain places in Atlanta because he's colored. He's not a real Southerner like we are. He came from Ohio to live here with his aunt when his mother died and he wasn't much more than a milk-tooth kid. Young as he was when he came, he knowed it was different down here, and he feels it worse and worse. Him and Joyce used to talk a lot about moving up to Cleveland to live, and I was all but glad when they did. I was afraid some day it would come to pass he'd get in trouble down here, the way he feels, and he'd done got Joyce in the same mind.

He even votes, which he says it never did him no good to

vote in Atlanta. He keeps on at me about it takes a hundred
and seventy votes in Fulton County to add up to one vote
in Echols County, and I just don't see how that could be.
That's the foolishest kind of adding up I ever heard tell
of. I don't know what is this county unit system he takes
on about, and I wish he'd let me alone. He picks at me to
register and vote my own self, and I don't know why does
he want me to vote if the votes don't count noway. I'm
well experienced in most things, but not voting, and Gerald gets real worrisome about all this.

When he runs his tongue and carries on a lot of that
nonsense though, I can't help but remember Poppa and
how he used to shake his head and say: "The day will
come . . ." Mr. Talmadge, before this election, said them
Negroes that was wise would make sure to stay away from
the polls. Well, Poppa was real wise, and I know he
wouldn't have helt on to a plumb foolish notion. Yet and
still, Momma always felt if you kept your mouth shut, you
wouldn't get no flies in it. So when they come back down
here to visit and Gerald starts at me like that—which he
don't miss a time—I just get all bumfoozled. I've lived the
biggest portion of my life without getting in no trouble
with white folks, and I don't want to start now.

I thought to my soul Gerald would bust a gut when we
got them first colored policemen in Atlanta.

That first Saturday afternoon the colored policemen

met at the Butler Street YMCA before they went out on their first beat. They were all eight of them lined up to go out at four o'clock, and the street was solid with people that had come to see them.

There they were all lined up and the Chief was telling each one what neighborhood he wanted him to go in. They were going to have beats on Auburn Avenue, Decatur Street, and other places where most of the colored people live at. Quite naturally, all us wanted to see them when they started out. I was due to be at work that day, but I plain out laid off and went to see the policemen.

One old lady carried them a big bouquet and said she wanted to beautify their office. She took the flowers ahead of time, and they took the bouquet inside and put it on a desk. She shook hands with each one of the new colored policemen and said: "God bless you all," and she was all but crying. And another lady come later with flowers and passed them out to all the policemen just as they started out on their beats. I know they'd have felt like ninnyhammers going on duty with a flower in their hand though. They just carried them down the street a little piece so as not to hurt her feelings, and then gave them to some children.

Auburn Avenue was sure like a parade that afternoon. For one thing, the Salvation Army band was playing on the corner of Auburn and Bell. That was the first time the Salvation Army had come in the colored section, and that drew a big crowd right by itself. And then the colored policemen just a block or so away—just hundreds and hundreds were out to see them. For a while white policemen on motorcycles went up and down the street keeping it a little bit clear, but finally not even the motorcycle cops could get through. You just couldn't get up or down Auburn Avenue noway.

Some of the people that came were so far away—the crowd was so thick—that they couldn't see any of the policemen until the Chief went off with one of them. There was this one great big black one, and the Chief taken him in his own car way out Piedmont.

Some of them that didn't get to see the policemen lined up, when they saw the Chief had one in his car, they just tore out and went to running right behind the car. The car couldn't hardly move without running people over, so for a while they could almost keep up with it. When it did get to where the car could move along some, they couldn't last long but they run after it till they got left behind. Somebody asked them how come they did that, and they said they hadn't got to see all the policemen lined up and so they sure wanted a good look at this one.

The other policemen had beats closer around to the Y; and when they started out walking, the people crowded around them so they could hardly move. Everybody kept asking them what their names were. What it was, everybody kept hoping some of them would have parents they'd know. That did happen with some, especially one policeman whose father used to work for the city in his lifetime

and was well known. All the people what did find policemen with parents they knew, even if they just hardly knew
them by sight and wasn't acquainted with them at all,
they'd go around saying: "Did you see young So-and-So?
Well, he's So-and-So's boy."

It was a regular parade up and down Auburn all right,
with everybody just bugging their eyes out at the colored
policemen. All around me I'd hear this: "You been to see
the policemen?"

"Not yet."

"Well, run on down there—some of them's still on Auburn."

My friend Sarah said when she got there they were gone.
A man told her some of them had gone out toward Piedmont, and she struck out again and went plumb to Peachtree and Auburn. She didn't think to look in any place of
business, just on the street, and when she got back—telling everybody she'd missed them and how far she'd gone
—they said: "Why, there's two of them right in the Yeah
Man Cafe drinking Coca-Cola."

She was so tired she just fell in the door, and she looked
so foolish that a man asked her what was the matter. She
said: "Nothing. I'm just looking for them colored police,
and I been all up to Auburn to Yates and Milton, to Piedmont and back down Auburn again. I'm plumb wore out."

Nobody didn't have to tell her again, because while she
was talking she saw them sitting at the wiener counter
right in front of her face. She went to a table and ordered

a Coca-Cola and got a good long look at them while she was drinking it. She knew they'd heard her, but they just laughed.

While she was there, stretching out that Coca-Cola long as she could, somebody else come in looking. When he saw the policemen he stuck his head back out the door and called to a crowd in the street: "Here they are in here!" and then they all come a-piling in. They filled up that little old wiener joint right then.

The police looked like they were getting embarrassed at people staring at them, Sarah said. They got up and stretched and started out, and everybody there started out right behind them. Sarah—and she's as big as my circulator heater—was in that crowd too, and pushing. When the whole bunch of them got out on the street, the police stood there awhile on the sidewalk and talked to some of them. Then back down Auburn they started back walking on their beat, the two of them together, and that crowd of children and grown folks right behind them.

Everybody was so interested because they never had in all their born days seen a colored policeman. They were so proud and glad of it. I reckon they thought they wouldn't be beat up and mistreated any more, and that these wouldn't do them as bad as the white policemen. (I don't know is it true or not, but folks do tell it—both white and colored folks—that lots of the white Atlanta policemen is Klansmen. I heard tell that one time the Klan give Herman Talmadge a big rich-looking car, a Cadillac or some such, and that it was an Atlanta policeman what made the giving-away speech.) Anyhow, that's why these colored folks kept dogging the colored policemen's footsteps. And they followed them around that way for more than a month.

One woman—I disremember her name, but she's the biggest clowner in Atlanta—was so proud of the colored policemen that she wanted to be the first somebody to be arrested by one. She talked to them real nice at first—she couldn't help but be rejoicing over them—and she asked where all their beats would be, and they told her. She said she knew they'd get plenty of trade down there. She said: "Because you all know where the crooked work is going on," and they said yes, they knew right sharp about it.

She asked this big hefty one: "How you think you're going to like being a policeman?" He said he hoped and reckoned he'd like it fine, and then she went to mouthing and teasing at him. She made like she knew him—which of course she never clapped eyes on him before—and she said: "Well, if you don't do any better at it than you did at the last job you had, you won't keep it long." Long about here it had come back to her that she'd planned to be the first one carried down, so she kept on picking at him.

When he'd tell her to go on away, she'd holler and stomp her feet and run right up to his face. "You make me go! You're the law! Now you just make me go!" She'd had a shot or two but she wasn't noways drunk. But he said: "Why don't you go on home and sleep it off? I don't want to lock you up."

She went to raising sand then. "Lock me up!" she hollered. "You *can't* lock me up! I just wish you'd try!" Then she told him his suit was tacky and he had on an old fifteen-cents cap, and called him a big old something—I couldn't hear exactly what she said. She was trying to make him mad so he'd arrest her.

He didn't realize what she was raising all this ruckus for, and when she just kept it up, calling him out of his name and all, he grabbed her by the arm and marched her down to the Y, to the little headquarters.

A white policeman, the one that called the wagon, said: "Aren't you ashamed to get yourself arrested just the first crack out of the box these boys get to work?" She just fell out laughing and slapped her hands together like she was at a revival meeting. She said: "No, God, I ain't. I did that on purpose to get arrested. I wanted to be the first somebody in Atlanta to be arrested by a colored policeman."

The wagon came and got her, but she was back in less than half an hour. Somebody went down and put up the twelve dollars for her—he had took up a collection from all us right there on the street—and got her right out. She came back laughing, and she's been bragging ever since.

The other night on Forrest Avenue a man and his wife—which they do fight all the time—went on worse than they ever did before. He carried on so loud that they finally both got arrested. His friends told him later he shouldn't have cut up like that, that he'd never done so bad as to be arrested before. He said he really was sort of sorry he got actually arrested, and he would purely hate to be arrested by a white policeman, but he didn't really feel so tore up by being arrested since it was a colored man did it. He said: "Even if I was on my way to the jail, which such a thing never happened to me before in my life, I felt like a citizen. It made a power of difference to me that if I had to get arrested it was a colored policeman carrying me down."

And one Saturday Joe, that's Viola's boy friend, got so mad he could have spit if he didn't have better manners. On his way to our place, he saw a crowd bigger than a circus on the corner of Mitchell and Davis. He thought sure something had done happened, and he run two long blocks to see. When he got there and pushed through the crowd, wasn't nothing to see but two colored policemen leaning up against a wall and everybody standing around staring at them.

I'm real proud of them myself. Onliest thing what worried me when they first come on the force, I didn't want anybody to hurt any of those colored policemen. I hoped wouldn't any colored men be so evil and jealous because they didn't get the opportunity themselves. The bluesuits have to pass a lot of tests and things, and couldn't just anybody do it. I knowed no white folks would bother them, because they don't have anything to do with the white folks. No matter what the colored policemen see white folks doing, they don't have anything to do with it. Gerald went to snorting and pawing about this even. He said a policeman ought to be a policeman; and if one saw somebody breaking the law, was he white or black or green and pink stripedy, the policeman ought to could arrest him. I just don't pay Gerald no mind when he talks like this. Still and yet, later it comes back to me and I go to wondering.

I think quite naturally it's a good thing to have these colored policemen. I think when they come in people's houses maybe they won't go ahead and tear up the place the way the white ones used to. When the police think you're writing for the bug, some of them used to turn everything in the house upside down, even dump flour out of a can on the floor, Lord, they was awful. I believe the colored ones would come in and look, but I don't believe they'd dump your flour on the floor or rip the mattress all to pieces. I don't believe they'd come in and beat people up, and I don't believe they'd bring in a number on a slip of paper and drop it on the floor and make like they found it there.

Gerald and me talked a lot to each other about the colored policemen, because Gerald is real serious-minded about a lot of things. Still and yet, he's young and frolicsome too. He's a snappy dresser, and his face brights up when he talks, and he plays his Frank Sinatra records, and he likes to have fun. Him and Joyce sure put the little pot in the big pot the night of their two-years' anniversary. They went to Henry's Cabaret—it's the swellest place in Atlanta that colored people have—and they sure put on the dog.

I went there once. You don't pay nothing to go in downstairs, but you sure got to turn loose your dough upstairs. The man that owns it is making money by the load.

There was four couples outside of Joyce and Gerald, and one extra boy. They went upstairs, and they was just surrounded with tables. Viola wore a thin dress, one of these skirts made in three ruffles and full like an evening dress. I made Joyce a black-and-white checked suit, and she sure looked like a tailor-made chicken. Both of them had on corsages, two-fifty apiece. Gerald had on his beautiful gray suit and a black tie. They'd all rather dress up than eat pound cake.

All these young folks got to where they're having anniversaries now, and Gerald had told me he wanted to do more big-shot things than the rest of them had did. He said he wanted me to give him some ideas about what to do. I said: "Now, if you want to be a big shot sure enough, you call Horace Richardson. He's the one got the new Chrysler or some kind of big car and he runs it for a taxi. You tell him you're having an anniversary party at Henry's Cabaret and you want him to do your hauling." They made it up that Horace would park on Auburn right in front of the cabaret at two o'clock, for them to leave.

They all met at my place, and they had these cashew nuts and potato chips and olives sitting around on tables. Some of them had been drinking, but they wasn't high. Then Gerald pulled his big idea on them. When him and me talked about it before the party, he said: "I'm going to make them sick with this. When Lawrence had his anniversary he had some fifths of whisky, and they made big old ugly bundles. I've got a better idea."

So when they were about ready to leave, Gerald went back and got the whisky out of my linen closet where he'd put it. He had half a pint for each one of the men. When he gave them the bottles, their eyes got big as hen eggs. They put the bottles in their hip pockets, and they all sashayed down the steps to start to Henry's.

Time they got there they went to dancing—before they even sat down. Them that was sort of high started it. Viola and the other sober ones would just as soon have eaten first. Anyhow, they danced first and then they went to the tables. They all said it was the best food they ever popped a lip over, excusing my sweet-potato pie.

That was the first time Viola had ever been to a place like that, and she said afterwards: "Momma, you should have seen me prissing up there to the fountain to get some water." She didn't have to, of course. The waiter would have brought it to her. But she wanted that deep lace on her petticoat to show, so she'd switch over and get the water at the fountain.

After they got through eating, they went back to the dance hall. In there, there was a floor show and singing and dancing, and a bouquet of flowers was on all the tables. All the couples danced, and everybody but my children was high as Georgia pines.

When they were coming out at two o'clock they saw Horace waiting for them with the Chrysler. He's a good-looking man, his eyes sparkle like diamonds and the women are just wild in the head about him. Some of those women won't ride with anybody else, Horace is so pretty. They were all calling: "Oh, there's Horace," and "Here's that sweet man," and "Here's the man what's going to carry me home," and all such as that. Horace said he was sorry, he was engaged and had six couples to haul. Quite naturally my crowd felt pretty big then, and Gerald come stepping out. He had paid a quarter for him a cigar, and he was smoking it by this time. He never smokes cigars except when he wants to act big; what he is is a cigarette smoker. I wish I'd been there; I'd have bought a ticket to see them cutting the fool that night.

So Gerald come stepping out, smoking his cigar, and he said: "Where is all my guests at? Come on, everybody. Here's Horace and the taxi." The girls all went on down and the men right behind them. White and colored police-men were standing around—the white policemen check everybody in and out, and if you haven't got one of those stubs when you come out they know you done slipped in. One of these white policemen said to Gerald: "You all sure do look nice, and you sure are a lovely bunch of colored people. That's what we like, and we hope more like you will come back." Gerald said he felt richer that night than he ever felt in his life.

Gerald and Joyce didn't go home. Gerald wasn't studying about going home. Him and Joyce come to my place and stayed all night with me and Viola. Gerald would have bust wide open if he hadn't got to tell me how he made them all sick. When they come home I was asleep, and the first thing I knowed Gerald had his arms around me and was just kissing me and saying: "You's the sweetest mother. You ain't no mother-in-law—you're a *mother*. You sure did help me pull this party, and gee, I felt big. You should have seen me ordering my guests out, telling them where to sit down, what car to take, and you're the cause of all that. I can't help from loving you." I knowed he was high as a kite, and I said: "If you don't get out of here I'm going to take my shoe and knock you in the head."

He sat down by the bed and said: "Wake up, Mrs. Workman, I want to tell you something. Because you helped me pull this party and everything went so swell, you know what I'm going to do? I'm going to pay for your teeth. You go on ahead to that dentist and get them teeth. I'll pay for them."

Saturday morning I said: "Gerald, are you still riding

those white horses?" He said: "No, I'm not, and I remember what I said about your teeth, and I meant it. I'll pay for them. I want to. I'm tired of seeing you suffer without them." So after he got it started, I jumped to the telephone, and two days later I was at the dentist's.

It took a right smart while to get the balance of my teeth out and my plates made; and by the time I got my new teeth, Joyce and Gerald had gone to Cleveland to live. They've made some very nice friends there—which of course Gerald still has kinfolks there to make them acquainted—and he holds down a good job and they have a nice place to live in. Gerald calls himself a refugee from Georgia, and he ain't just talking to fan the breeze.

7

No, Gerald ain't just running his tongue. The cause of his hauling out of Georgia was that he couldn't get a job. Oh, he could find work all right, but why should he be somebody's yard man when he knowed how to be a postal clerk? I never minded hiring out to work in white folks' houses, myself. I minded the way the biggest portion of them treated their help, but still and yet I didn't know how to do no other kind of work. Many a night I hated to see the next morning come, because of the place I was working at, but it was all the kind of work I knew how to do.

With Gerald it's different. Lots of these young folks has had chances I never did, and I knew the first time Gerald come to our place delivering the *Atlanta Journal* that any chance he had in life he'd take it. He used to bounce in here, bold and bright as a jay bird; and you could tell to look at him he wasn't just sassy, he was smart. He made out very well in school, and I reckon he'd have made out very well in college if he'd had the chance to get there.

When he got older and began to get better jobs than the paper route, he made a good record wherever he worked. He learned things easy, and he was always swift to get his work done. And when he went in the Army, he made a good record there too. While he was in the Army, he learned how to do this postal clerking, and all the time he was overseas he was looking to get a job in the Post Office when he come back home.

I just preached to him about how it wasn't no use and he'd just be making trouble for all us here if he kept on and kept on about going to work at the Post Office, but he wouldn't budge one smidgin. "I got my eyes open now," he said. "I knew all along it was all wrong, but now I've been in other places and met people from all kinds of places—and Negroes don't live other places like they do in Georgia. And you never get anywhere if you don't try."

And he just kept on at the Post Office to give him that job. He took his civil-service examinations, which he did very well on them, he said, but every time he'd pester them about a job they'd wangle and twist and get out of it some way. Of course the lump in the sauce was that he was colored. I knowed he was right when he said that. Everybody knowed it.

And if the truth was told, everybody'd know it's on account of the same thing I couldn't get me that washing-machine and adopt that child.

For a right smart while I had it in mind to adopt little Cherokee Williams, which his mother would have been tickled if I had—the Williamses got so many children they can't hardly keep their bodies and souls together. Cherokee ain't a day more than three years old, but that little buster knows just as good how to find his way down around the court to my place and tromp up this long flight of stairs to the second floor where we live at.

It had done got to where I looked out after him so much I might as well have kept him. On top of that, I knowed it was for me to keep him either his mother would give him to some of her kinfolks down in Climax. It wasn't that Mary Martha didn't love him—he's a sweet child and couldn't nobody keep from loving him—but they plain out can't feed that many mouths, and Cherokee was all the time getting the short end of things anyhow.

Not too long back he come wandering up here one evening, hot as a pistol and shiny-eyed with fever and his nose all running and everything. I give him a lukewarm bath and some aspirin and put him to bed, and the first child I seen going by in the court I hollered out the window and told him to tell Cherokee's mother he'd be along home when I had done got him well.

I kept him the whole week-end, which it wasn't any trouble, I already had some little clothes for him. He used to come in all dirty so much that I'd sent Viola down to Grant's and got him some little marked-down things. I always did like for him to come. He's got the best disposition, and he's pretty enough for a calendar baby. He's got that nice round head, and a good straight back, and the neatest little navel scar. No Elberta peach that ever grew in Fort Valley is prettier than that boy.

Some of these folks around here claim he's named Cherokee on account he's got some Indian blood in him, but it ain't a word of truth in it. His mother named him out of the telephone book, and she did it in my kitchen before he was born. She come up to borrow my phone when she was just hardly pregnant, and she called up her white folks to say she was poorly and couldn't make it to work that day. Their phone was on the Cherokee exchange, and seemed like that word had a good sound to her. She said she'd name the baby Cherokee, she liked it so well, and it wouldn't hinder her none if the baby was a boy or either a girl. And that's how it came about, no matter what's talked around by these folks what has their tongues tied in the middle and loose at both ends.

Well, I made up my mind to adopt him. Not by law, but just keep him here with me. I knowed it would be all right with his mother before I even brought it up to her. I studied about how could I do it, and it came to me that if I could some way get a washing-machine and take in laundries—why, I could manage. That way I could quit my day work and be home to see after Cherokee. So I took to watching the ads in the papers. Every morning I'd borrow the *Constitution* from some of the neighbors, and I'd look in my own *Journal* every evening. I sent word to the Baptist preacher, and told everybody in the project I was looking for me a washing-machine. Nothing ever come of it, but one of my white folks wrote off to *Strike It Rich* about me and how I needed a washer.

Finally I found it. A good second-handed washing-machine. It was a wringer washer, just what I wanted. These fancyfaluted ones is nice to use—they really are just as handy as a pocket in a shirt—but they go to breaking down all the time, and you have to be rich as a county commissioner to keep one going. I jumped right to the phone when I seen that ad and talked to the lady. I told her I'd need a week to get the money, but I sure did want that washer. At first she wouldn't pay me no mind, but I went to telling her about Cherokee and how I'd have to borrow the money from my married daughter in Cleveland and all. I really ran my tongue, and, when she found out all about how it was, she come down real nice and said all right, she'd wait for one week, but no more.

I made Viola write to Joyce that night for me and then go all the way to the Post Office to get the letter in the mail that very same night. All that while I was waiting to hear from her, I was planning on things to do for Cherokee. He could sleep on the sofa in the living-room—he was plenty big enough not to fall off—and I could make him lots of little clothes without hardly spending anything, and I could take him to see the fountain at Hurt Park when it's all different colors at night. I like to died right side of my mail box when I opened the letter from Joyce and seen she had done sent me a check.

I don't know whether she had done lived up there so long she purely acted like a Yankee or either had she done it to show off to her Yankee friends, but ain't a colored person in Georgia wouldn't have known what a worrisome thing a check is. It come on a Saturday afternoon, and I only had till that night to pay for the washer. I tracked all over the curb market that afternoon with my check, but it didn't do a bit of good because I'm not known there. I went from one stall to the other till closing time, and wouldn't a Lord's soul cash my check for me. Time I drug myself on back home I was just crying down.

Whenever I could get my face straight, I phoned up the lady and asked her would she wait till Monday for the money, but she said no, she couldn't. She talked nice enough, but I could tell she didn't believe I had no check. She said she had to get rid of that machine on account of some other plans of her own and she had done kept somebody waiting, and, since I didn't get the money to her when I said I would, she'd have to let this couple have it.

With that, I went to feeling just like Gerald. When him and Joyce got completely fed up with the way things is here, he quit that tookie little job in the filling-station and they sold that nice new house in Dixie Hills and took their selves up North. And now I'm leaving too. The Bible says there's a time to plant and a time to pluck up; I guess there's a time to hold still and a time to get a move on. I'm packing up my stuff and I'm getting out of Georgia like a bat out of torment. Folks can talk all they want about never getting this Georgia red clay off your shoes, but I'm getting it off mine and it's going to stay off. I don't want no more truck with this state, never.

Mean and hateful as she is, Joyce is my natural-born child, and I didn't appreciate her having to move clean to Ohio so Gerald could get him a decent job. That's been sticking in my craw all this while, and these other things coming all in a heap is too much for flesh and blood to put up with. First they do all those evil, low-down things to keep anybody my color from voting; then they shoot Cousin Walter to death with his wife and kids for eyeball witnesses; and then Mrs. Carruthers talking like I was too dirty to breathe the same air as her and her family.

Nothing ever flew all over me the way that did about her bed. Telling me I needn't sleep on a pallet, just go ahead and be comfortable and sleep in the guest room, she was going to get the mattress cleaned and re-covered anyhow. I wonder what was she aiming to do with the sheets —burn them? And I wonder how come little Don stays fit for her to touch. I've knowed that child since he was an arm baby. I've changed his diapers, and fixed his bottles, and rocked him to sleep—which Mrs. Curruthers would just stick him in the crib wide awake—and give him his medicine when he was sick. I don't see how does she figure I'm clean enough to do all this but too dirty to sleep in a bed in her house.

And now little Cherokee's with his aunt in South Georgia and I've done lost him before I even really had him.

This is exactly the same as that one time I went to the seashore, down at Jacksonville, and fast as I'd hardly half-way get up from being knocked flat by one wave, glory be to the Father, here'd come another one and knock me flat again. Joyce leaving . . . Cousin Walter . . . Mrs. Carruthers . . . Cherokee . . . and now this election. This election is the crowner.

Georgia is my own home. I was birthed here, and so was all my children, and I all along looked to die here. But I ain't going to live through no other Talmadge. I don't understand why we got to keep on having Talmadges for governors, and I ain't going to try. I'm just going to put my foot in my hand and get out of here. I ain't going to leave nothing behind me with breath in the body that's kin to me. I'm going to take Viola, and my first cousin, and Florrie and John D., and, praise God, Joyce and Gerald are already gone. Miss Fay'll get me a job, and I can't help but believe things'll be better in Washington. I been ready in my mind to go since they shot Cousin Walter —his own wife left right after that happened—and now Mrs. Carruthers pulled that low-down trick on me, I *am* going.

I don't care, either. I reckon I ought to feel sad at my age to leave the state where I was born and lived all my life and raised my family, but I can't keep on feeling like it's my home if these Talmadge people are going to run everything again. I don't want to see never another birthday in this state. I'm fed up.

Viola ain't being a bit of help. She's just digging her heels in and pulling back like a bully calf. Every day she comes home from her job and just about aggravates me to death trying to get me to unpack what I worked myself down during the day to get boxed up. I don't know what's got into Viola. All her life she's been the most biddable child you could think of; and here now, at a time like this, she acts up worse than Joyce. And Florrie and John D. ain't no better. Florrie says she'll do whatever John D. says do, and John D. just says cold out he ain't going. First off he listened to me and we was all going, but then he got mulish about it, and now that tomfool has done gone down to the courthouse and registered to vote in the next go-round. It appears to me like everybody but me has gone stark staring crazy.

Well, they can just stay. I moved to Atlanta without help from any of them, and I'll move plumb out of Georgia without them if they're bound to act crazy as Betsy bugs. If they want to stay here in this hornet's nest and find their selves dead in a ditch some day, with John D. voting and all that foolishness, I ain't going to be here to see it.

Still and yet, both John D. and Gerald put me in mind of Poppa some way. A gooder man than Poppa never walked the earth, and he never got into no trouble with white folks all his livelong days. But I can see him right now, dreaming about colored folks voting—which we all thought he was out of his mind at the time, and it scared us stiff as an ironing-board every time he did it—dreaming about it and tapping his fist in his other palm and saying: "The day will come. . . ." I reckon he knew he was done thinking ahead of his times, because he sure never let on to anybody but us, white or colored, what was in the back of his mind.

Whilst I pack up my stuff I keep coming across things my good white friends gave me, and that sets me to thinking again. This morning I was putting all my special and fine underwear in a box by itself—presents, all of it, and never been worn—and I took out those yellow silk step-ins Miss Fay gave me. They're none of this slick, slippy, slidy nylon, but pure silk, and the prettiest pale yellow—just the color of creamery butter—with ecru lace as deep as ruffles on real sissy bedroom curtains.

They're just beautiful, and they're real scandalous looking. They cost like fire, I know, and couldn't nobody but a kept woman really wear that kind of thing. I don't know why, but I'd rather get that kind of a present than eat pound cake. I set here and laughed out loud all by myself thinking about when Mr. Bob went and bought them. It was for a Christmas present for me and Miss Fay had the bronchitis or something and couldn't go, and she sent Mr. Bob. He's not real squeamish the way some men are about buying women's things, but he said he did nearly have a running fit in Davison's before he got these things bought and got out with them. He said he absolutely will-powered himself into not having a fit because he couldn't stand the thought of the saleslady calling the floorwalker and saying (out loud for everybody to hear): "A man is having a fit in lady's underwear!" He was only funning, of course, but it did get him churned around; because time he got to my place with them step-ins, he was still red in the face and so mad he couldn't hardly wish me a Merry Christmas. Still and yet, he had taken them up on the mezzanine and got them gift-wrapped. He told me I was a Jezebel at heart or I wouldn't even want such as that, and Miss Fay had no proper regard for him else she wouldn't have sent him after them; but he didn't really mean it, he was just fussed up.

All my good dishes are packed up now, and the last things I put in were those tiny little thin china teacups and saucers Little Rodney Duke sent me from Japan when he was in the service. He remembered from when he was a small child how crazy I am about nice dishes. It's very fine ware and it's got a special name, but I disremember it. Six little bits of teacups and a saucer that exactly fits each one, and that red in the pattern is the prettiest shade. They don't look at all like the dishes you see around here, which naturally they wouldn't since they're from Japan.

I still have the card Little Rodney put in when he mailed them to me. It don't have none of his name on it, it just says: "For Willie Mae with fond good wishes from Her Boy." He always was affectionate. He hadn't been born yet when I first went to work for the Dukes—he wasn't hardly four when I married Dan—and now he's a man full growed I still can't call him anything but Little Rodney.

Then there's this little thingamajig in my sewing-box that I dearly love—it's some kind of a thing that makes a needle eye real big so you can see to thread it without no trouble. Mrs. Church brought it by here one day. It wasn't for no special reason, like a birthday or anything; she had just been downtown shopping and when she saw this thing it put her in mind of me. She knowed my eyes was going from bad to worse, and more than once she'd done seen me trying to thread a needle, and Lord knows I'd be poking that thread behind the eye and in front of the eye and over it and under it and every way in the world but through it. Since she give me this thing, I just slide that old thread right through the eye on the first try, good as if I had eyes like a hawk.

That's what was so nice about Mrs. Church. She'd *think* about you. Plenty of folks will give you something like at Christmas-time, even if it's a box of candy or a handkerchief because they don't want to fool with thinking up anything else, but not Mrs. Church. She'd give you some little something just whenever it come to her mind here was something you'd need or specially like, and that's why her presents always was the best presents—even if sometimes they didn't cost over fifty cents.

The thing that really turns my heart around in my chest though is this picture of all us here on my fiftieth birthday. I was putting all my pictures in a good stout Rich's box, and I ran up on this one Mr. David taken on my birthday. It's just as clear, and there we all are, right here in this kitchen, Joyce and Gerald, and Viola and her boyfriend, and Florrie and John D., and good old Dora, and me in the middle blowing out the candles on the cake Viola made me.

Mr. David was working at Emory then, teaching something about newspapering, and him and Miss Caroline come out here on my birthday and he had borrowed one of those highfaluted cameras what newspapers use to take their pictures with. That's how come the picture is so good and clear. I was so happy that day, and I wasn't the onliest one either. The man across the court was setting on his stoop when they come, and I was out front to meet them, and he just bugged his eyes out at us. I made them take one picture outdoors so everybody could see my white company. This man set there and watched the whole thing—which of course that was the only part he could see, not the cake and all indoors—and when Miss Caroline and Mr. David left, he followed after them down to the street, and they got in their car and he watched them out of sight.

Then he came back and said to me: "Miss Willie Mae—"

He's every bit as old as I am, but he's old-timey and he calls people Miss So-and-So. He said: "Miss Willie Mae, they's the nicest-acting white folks I ever saw." I was sure feeling my importance that day, and I said: "Sure they is. They's the best people in Georgia now the Cliffords is in Washington." He said: "Who is they? Your folks you work for?" I told him: "No, I don't work for them, they's just my friends. I met them at the Cliffords." And I went to work to make him sick. "I hadn't known them but two weeks," I told him, "when my eyes went bad on me. And they gave me twenty dollars in cash for my glasses, and they let me pay them back a quarter and fifty cents at the time, just whenever I could."

He wouldn't let my bragging get his goat though. He kept talking real serious and wondering like. He said: "I never did see white folks talk and act like them around people like us. I know I didn't have no part in this birthday picture-taking and they didn't even know I was watching, but to see them and you all like that together, them coming to your house and all—it made me feel like a human being myself. You is lucky to know them, and you better never let go of friends like that."

Well . . . now I think of it . . . I don't believe I will. They say one swallow don't make a drunk, and I reckon even two Talmadges don't make a Georgia. This here Georgia's my home place too, and I ain't going to run out of it like a tuck-tail dog.

Viola don't know it, but she's going to be a voter. I'm

too old to learn my own self. I've been drove hard and put up wet, and I'm too wore out to learn all what I'd have to, which you do have to keep up and know right smart about things if you vote. But Viola's young and quick, and I'm going to see she learns how to vote if I have to stand over her with a mop handle. All the other young sprouts in this housing-project too. I'm going to take out after them hot as a firecracker, and them as don't learn how and then go vote will have me to face. And they ain't hankering to stir me up; they'd just as soon fight a circle saw. Old I may be, and done got skinny and drawed up with the rheumatism; but one thing, they know I mean well by them, and another thing, I'm the hatefullest talking somebody in this project when I'm mad. And mad is what I am now.

Still and yet, I ain't feeling as burdensome as I did. I'm going to stir my stumps here and fix Viola a real good supper, and then I'll make her help me unpack all this stuff after we eat. I'll have her a nice hot pone of cornbread—which she'd rather eat cornbread than have a date on Saturday night—and I'll fry us a chicken and I think I'll even make a sweet-potato pie.

ELIZABETH LARISEY KYTLE was born in Charleston, South Carolina, and lived there until she was twelve, when she and her parents moved to Valdosta, Georgia. A graduate of the Georgia State Womans college (now Valdosta State College), she later lived in Atlanta, then Columbus, Ohio, and Washington, D.C. Since 1969 she and her husband, Calvin Kytle, have lived in Cabin John, Maryland. Her other books include *Four Cats Make One Pride*, for which she also took the photographs; *Home on the Canal*, an informal history of the old Chesapeake and Ohio Canal, followed by reminiscences of eleven men and women who lived and worked on the boats; and *The Voices of Robby Wilde*, the story of a paranoid schizophrenic.